CW01335576

African Recipes

An African Cookbook with Delicious African Recipes for All Types of Meals

By
BookSumo Press

Published by
http://www.booksumo.com

ENJOY THE RECIPES?

KEEP ON COOKING
WITH 6 MORE FREE COOKBOOKS!

Visit our website and simply enter your email address to join the club and receive your 6 cookbooks.

http://booksumo.com/magnet

https://www.instagram.com/booksumopress/

https://www.facebook.com/booksumo/

LEGAL NOTES

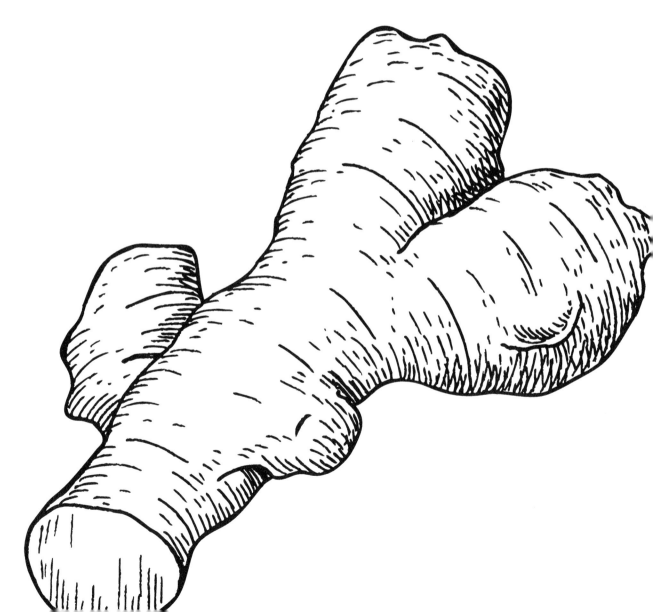

Table of Contents

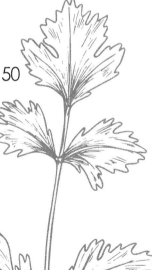

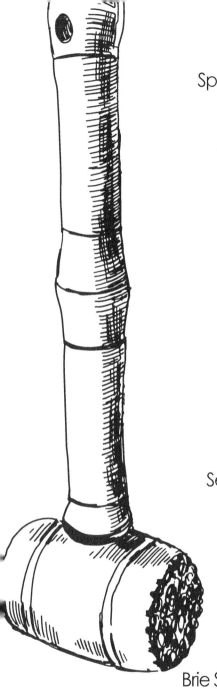

Paprika
Cayenne Glazed Wings

Prep Time: 10 mins
Total Time: 50 mins

Servings per Recipe: 3
Calories   710 kcal
Fat   46.9 g
Carbohydrates   43.7g
Protein   28 g
Cholesterol   136 mg
Sodium   2334 mg

Ingredients

oil for deep frying
1 C. unbleached all-purpose flour
2 tsps salt
1/2 tsp ground black pepper
1/2 tsp cayenne pepper
1/4 tsp garlic powder
1/2 tsp paprika
1 egg

1 C. milk
3 skinless, boneless chicken breasts, strips
1/4 C. hot pepper sauce
1 tbsp butter

Directions

1. Get your oil hot for frying. At the same time get a bowl, combine: paprika, flour, garlic powder, salt, cayenne, and black pepper.
2. Get a 2nd bowl, combine: milk and eggs. Coat your chicken first with the gg mix then dredge them in the flour mix.
3. Place the chicken back in the egg mix and again in the flour mix.
4. Place everything in a bowl and place a covering of plastic on the bowl. Put the chicken in the fridge for 30 mins then begin to fry the chicken, in batches, for 8 mins.
5. Once all the chicken is done get a 3rd bowl and combine your butter and hot sauce.
6. Place the mix in the microwave for 1 min with a high level of heat then top the chicken with the mix.
7. Enjoy.

AFRICAN HONEY
Beef Hot Pot

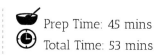

Prep Time: 45 mins
Total Time: 53 mins

Servings per Recipe: 6

Calories	1823.1
Fat	168.6g
Cholesterol	224.7mg
Sodium	325.9mg
Carbohydrates	56.7g
Protein	24.1g

Ingredients

3 lbs. organic beef, trimmed of fat & cubed
1 tbsp olive oil
1 lb. onion, peeled & quartered
4 -6 garlic cloves, peeled & chopped
1 lb. carrot, peeled & cut into chunks
9 oz. canned tomatoes
4 oz. dates, pitted but kept whole
6 oz. prunes, pitted but kept whole

2 tbsp honey
1/2 pint beef stock
1 cinnamon stick
6 tsp ras el hanout spice mix
salt & pepper
2 oz. toasted sliced almonds
2 tbsp fresh coriander, chopped

Directions

1. Bring a salted pot of water to a boil. Cook in it the carrots for 5 min. Drain them and place them aside.
2. Preheat the crock pot. Heat in it 2 tsp of olive oil. Sauté in it the onion for 3 min. Stir in the garlic with carrots.
3. Stir 1/2 pint of boiling water with 1 stock cube until it dissolves. Mix in it the honey with dry spices, honey, and cinnamon stick.
4. Stir the mixture into the pot with tomato, prunes and dates.
5. Place a large pan over medium heat. Heat in it 2 tsp of oil. Cook in it the beef dices for 3 to 5 min until they become golden brown.
6. Stir the browned beef into the crock pot with a pinch of salt and pepper. Put on the lid and let them cook for 8 to 11 h on low.
7. Spoon the beef stew over some hot couscous. Garnish it with some parsley, and toasted almonds. Serve your tagine warm.
8. Enjoy.

Ginger, Sweet Potato, and Peanut Butter Stew

Prep Time: 10 mins
Total Time: 30 mins

Servings per Recipe: 4

Calories	325.5
Fat	20.0g
Cholesterol	0.0mg
Sodium	356.7mg
Carbohydrates	31.4g
Protein	10.7g

Ingredients

3 C. stock
2 slices fresh ginger
1 sweet potato, peeled and chopped
2 carrots, chopped
1 yellow pepper, chopped
1/2 tsp cayenne
1 tbsp oil
2 onions, chopped

3 green onions, chopped
1 tbsp brown sugar
1/2 C. peanut butter
1 C. tomato juice
2 garlic cloves, chopped
salt and pepper

Directions

1. Place a saucepan over medium heat. Heat in it the oil. Cook in it the pepper, ginger, carrots, garlic, onions and cayenne or chilies for 3 min.
2. Stir in the stock with potato. Cook them until they start boiling. Let it cook for 12 min.
3. Transfer the mixture to a food blender. Blend them smooth.
4. Pour the soup back to the saucepan. Add to it the peanut butter with tomato juice, sugar, a pinch of salt and pepper.
5. Heat the soup for 1 to 2 min. Serve it warm.
6. Enjoy.

MOROCCAN
Kefta bites with Tomato Sauce

 Prep Time: 10 mins
Total Time: 35 mins

Servings per Recipe: 2
Calories	780.1
Fat	59.6g
Cholesterol	136.0mg
Sodium	166.0mg
Carbohydrates	22.1g
Protein	42.5g

Ingredients

Glaze
6 - 8 medium tomatoes, cored and chopped
1 tbsp paprika
1 tsp cumin
1/2 tsp cayenne pepper
3 - 4 tbsp chopped fresh flat - leaf parsley
2 garlic cloves, minced
salt & freshly ground black pepper,
1/4 C. vegetable oil

Meat
14 oz. ground beef
1 tbsp paprika
1 tsp cumin
1/2 tsp cayenne pepper
3 - 4 tbsp chopped fresh flat - leaf parsley
2 garlic cloves, minced
salt & freshly ground black pepper,

Directions

1. To make the sauce:
2. Place a tagine or a large pan over medium heat. Heat in it the oil. Add the remaining ingredients and stir them well.
3. Cook them for 16 min over low heat.
4. To make the meatballs:
5. Get a mixing bowl: Combine in it all the meatballs ingredients. Mix them well with your hands. Shape the mixture into medium sized meatballs. Place them over the sauce then put on the lid. Let them cook for 9 to 11 min. Serve your saucy meatballs tagine with some bread or spaghetti. Enjoy.

Moroccan
Midnight Hummus

🥣 Prep Time: 20 mins
🕐 Total Time: 2 hrs 20 mins

Servings per Recipe: 6

Calories	179.3
Fat	4.5g
Cholesterol	0.0mg
Sodium	799.9mg
Carbohydrates	29.0g
Protein	7.8g

Ingredients

1 C. dried garbanzo beans, soaked overnight
8 C. water
1 tbsp vegetable oil
2 C. onions, chopped
2 tomatoes, peeled and diced
8 garlic cloves, minced
1 small hot pepper, chopped

1/2 C. fresh coriander, leaf chopped
1/2 C. fresh flat leaf parsley, chopped
2 tsp salt
1 tsp fresh black pepper
1 lemon, juiced
1 tsp sweet paprika
1 tsp ground turmeric

Directions

1. Place a soup pot over medium heat. Stir in it the water with chickpeas. Bring them to a boil.
2. Put on the lid and let them cook for 60 min over low medium heat.
3. Place a small pan over medium heat. Heat in it the oil. Cook in it the onions, garlic, and hot pepper for 2 min.
4. Stir them into the chickpeas pot with the remaining ingredients. Put on half a lid, and cook the soup for an extra 60 min over low heat.
5. Serve your chickpea soup warm with some toasted tortilla strips.
6. Enjoy.

BAKED
Banana Splits

Prep Time: 5 mins
Total Time: 10 mins

Servings per Recipe: 6

Calories	189.1
Fat	5.9g
Cholesterol	0.0mg
Sodium	52.3mg
Carbohydrates	35.7g
Protein	1.5g

Ingredients

5 medium bananas
1 tbsp margarine, low-fat
1/3 C. orange juice
1 tbsp lemon juice

3 tbsp brown sugar, packed
2/3 C. shredded coconut

Directions

1. Before you do anything, preheat the oven to 375 F. Grease a baking dish with some butter.
2. Peel the bananas and cut them in half lengthwise. Slice each half into 2 pieces and lay them in the greased dish.
3. Top them with butte, orange and lemon juice. Cover them with the brown sugar and shredded coconut.
4. Place the pie in the oven and let it cook for 9 to 11 min. Serve it warm with some ice cream.
5. Enjoy.

Luanda
Piri Piri
(Chili Sauce)

Prep Time: 5 mins

Total Time: 1 hr 20 mins

Servings per Recipe: 1

Calories	692.0
Fat	70.6g
Cholesterol	0.0mg
Sodium	2468.4mg
Carbohydrates	17.6g
Protein	3.4g

Ingredients

4 tbsp lemon juice
5 tbsp olive oil
1/4 C. vinegar
1 tbsp cayenne pepper
1 tbsp garlic, minced

1 tbsp paprika
1 tsp salt
1 tbsp chili flakes

Directions

1. Before you do anything, preheat the oven to 450 F. Grease a baking sheet and place it aside.
2. Get a mixing bowl: Mix in it all the ingredients. Place the marinade in the fridge until ready to use.
3. Use this marinade to marinate chicken, fish, veggies or meat for at least 1 h before grilling or roasting, or baking them.
4. Enjoy.

AFRICAN
Peanut Butter Truffles

Prep Time: 15 mins
Total Time: 15 mins

Servings per Recipe: 1	
Calories	55.6
Fat	1.7g
Cholesterol	3.5mg
Sodium	14.4mg
Carbohydrates	9.6g
Protein	1.0g

Ingredients

1 C. low-fat peanut butter
1 C. honey, slightly warm
1 - 2 C. powdered milk

1/2 C. grated coconut

Directions

1. Before you do anything, preheat the oven to 450 F. Line up baking sheet with parchment paper.
2. Get a mixing bowl: Beat the honey with peanut butter until they become smooth.
3. Mix in 1 C. of powdered milk until you get a smooth dough. Shape the dough into bite size balls.
4. Coat the peanut butter balls with coconut. Place them on the lined up baking sheet.
5. Place the peanut butter bites in the fridge and cover them with piece of parchment paper.
6. Let them sit for at least 1 h then serve them.
7. Enjoy.

Broccoli Salad
with Honey Dressing

🥣 Prep Time: 15 mins
🕐 Total Time: 15 mins

Servings per Recipe: 6
Calories	227.8
Fat	18.1g
Cholesterol	19.9mg
Sodium	470.8mg
Carbohydrates	14.7g
Protein	5.3g

Ingredients

4 1/2 C. broccoli florets, small
2 1/2 C. cauliflower florets, small
1 1/2 C. carrots, sliced
1 tbsp canola oil
1 tsp salt
1 tsp ground ginger
1 tsp ground cumin
1/2 tsp ground coriander
1/2 tsp freshly ground nutmeg

1/2 tsp crushed red pepper flakes
1 C. sour cream
2 tbsp cider vinegar
1 tbsp mild honey
1/2 C. sliced green onion
1/2 C. toasted pine nuts

Directions

1. Prepare a steamer. Place in it the broccoli with carrots and cauliflower. Let them steam for 2 to 3 min covered.
2. Place them in some hot water then drain them and place them in a colander to dry.
3. Place a pan over medium heat. Stir in it the oil with ginger, cumin, coriander, nutmeg, red pepper flakes and salt. Let them cook for 1 to 2 min.
4. Get a mixing bowl: Whisk in it the cooked spice mixture, sour cream, vinegar, and honey to make the dressing.
5. Place the steamed veggies in a serving bowl. Drizzle over them the dressing and toss them to coat.
6. Garnish the salad with some green onion and toasted nuts then serve it.
7. Enjoy.

SOMALI INSPIRED
Rainbow Salad

Prep Time: 15 mins
Total Time: 15 mins

Servings per Recipe: 4
Calories   54.2
Fat   2.5g
Cholesterol   0.0mg
Sodium   152.5mg
Carbohydrates   7.8g
Protein   1.4g

Ingredients

2 C. ripe tomatoes, seeded & diced
1 1/2 C. cucumbers, diced
1/4 C. sweet onion, diced
1 green hot pepper, seeded and diced
4 tsp lemon juice
2 tsp balsamic vinegar

1/4 tsp salt
1/4 tsp pepper
2 tsp extra virgin olive oil

Directions

1. Get a mixing bowl: Toss in it all the salad ingredients.
2. Serve your salad right away.
3. Enjoy.

African Chicken Cutlets

🥣 Prep Time: 1 hr

🕐 Total Time: 1 hr 10 mins

Servings per Recipe: 6	
Calories	167.2
Fat	3.0g
Cholesterol	50.3mg
Sodium	223.5mg
Carbohydrates	14.6g
Protein	19.2g

Ingredients

4 boneless skinless chicken breasts, sliced
1 lemon, juice
1 small onion
salt & pepper

1 C. fine breadcrumbs
oil

Directions

1. Get a mixing bowl: Stir in the chicken slices with lemon juice, onion liquid, a pinch of salt and pepper.
2. Cover the bowl and place it in the fridge for at least 60 min.
3. Place a pan over medium heat. Heat in it a swirl of oil.
4. Drain the chicken slices from and coat them with the breadcrumbs.
5. Place some of the in the hot oil and cook them for 3 to 5 min on each side until they become golden brown.
6. Repeat the process with the remaining chicken slices. Serve your fried chicken with your favorite dip.
7. Enjoy.

ALMOND
Beef Casserole

🍲 Prep Time: 40 mins

🕐 Total Time: 1 hr 35 mins

Servings per Recipe: 4

Calories	634.7
Fat	34.9g
Cholesterol	223.6mg
Sodium	1450.9mg
Carbohydrates	39.2g
Protein	41.5g

Ingredients

1 1/2 lbs. ground beef
oil
2 slices white bread, torn into pieces
1/2 C. milk
1 large onions, chopped
4 tsp curry powder, mild
1 tbsp biriyani spices, crushed
1/2 tsp turmeric
1 tomatoes, ripe, peeled and chopped
1/2 tsp sugar
1 apple, peeled and grated

1 tbsp grated lemon rind
1/4-1/2 C. seedless raisin
2 tsp salt
2 tbsp apricot jam
1 egg
3/4 C. milk
12 -16 almonds, whole, blanched
1 egg, plus
1/2 C. milk
1/3 tsp turmeric

Directions

1. Before you do anything, preheat the oven to 350 F. Grease a baking dish and place it aside.
2. Get a mixing bowl: Stir in it 1/2 C. of milk with bread. Let them sit for few minutes.
3. Place a pan over medium heat. Heat in it 3 tbsp of oil. Cook in it the onion for 3 min.
4. Stir in the curry powder, crushed biriyani spices and turmeric. Cook for 1 to 2 min while adding more oil if needed.
5. Stir in the tomato, sugar, grated apple and lemon rind. Cook them for 1 min.
6. Stir in the meat with apricot jam and cook them for 3 min while stirring them all the time.
7. Turn off the heat and let the meat mixture cool down for few minutes.
8. Drain the bread pieces from the milk and squeeze them gently dry. Crumble them.
9. Get a mixing bowl: Mix in it the crumbled bread with the meat mixture.
10. Pour the mixture into the greased dish and spread it in an even layer. Top it with almonds.
11. Place the meatloaf dish in the oven and let it cook for 42 min.
12. Get a small mixing bowl: Mix in it the reserved milk with turmeric, and egg.

13. Pour the mixture over the meatloaf. Place it back in the oven and cook it for an extra 16 min.
14. Serve your meatloaf dish with some rice and your favorite toppings.
15. Enjoy.

FLAT BREAD
Addis Abba (Injera)

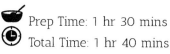

Prep Time: 1 hr 30 mins
Total Time: 1 hr 40 mins

Servings per Recipe: 15
Calories	119.4
Fat	0.5g
Cholesterol	0.0mg
Sodium	321.0mg
Carbohydrates	24.8g
Protein	3.6g

Ingredients

3 C. self-rising flour
1/2 C. whole wheat flour
1/2 C. cornmeal

1 tbsp active dry yeast
3 1/2 C. warm water

Directions

1. Get a mixing bowl: Combine in it all the ingredients. Mix them well.
2. Pour the mixture into a greased bowl and cover it. Let it rest for at least 2 h 30 min to 6 h 20 min to rise.
3. Get a food processor: Pour in it 2 C. of the batter. Blend it smooth with adding 1/2 to 3/4 C. of water to make the mixture thin.
4. Repeat the process with the remaining mixture until it becomes thin.
5. Place a large non-sticking skillet over medium heat. Pour in it 1/2 C. of the dough mixture in it.
6. Swirl the pan to cover it base with it. Let it cook over low medium heat until the batter sit and starts bubbling.
7. Flip it gently and let it cook until it become golden brown on both sides.
8. Repeat the process with the remaining batter. Serve your Ethiopian with whatever you desire.
9. Enjoy.

Abyssinian
Potato Stew

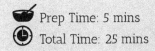

Prep Time: 5 mins
Total Time: 25 mins

Servings per Recipe: 1
Calories   189.9
Fat   5.3g
Cholesterol   0.0mg
Sodium   93.7mg
Carbohydrates   32.5g
Protein   5.6g

Ingredients

1/2 onion, diced
3 garlic cloves, minced
1 tsp fresh ginger, minced
1/2 small sweet potatoes, diced
1/4 red sweet bell pepper, diced
1 tsp olive oil
2 tbsp lentils
1 - 2 tsp tomato paste
1 C. water
3/4 tsp paprika

1/2 tsp ground coriander
1/4 tsp ground allspice
1/4 tsp ground cinnamon
1/4 tsp ground fenugreek
1/4 tsp ground ginger
salt
black pepper

Directions

1. Place a stew pot over medium heat. Heat in it the oil. Cook in it the onion, garlic, ginger and yam for 4 min.
2. Stir in the bell pepper and cook them for 2 min. Stir in the water with tomato paste and lentils.
3. Cook them until they start boiling. Stir in the paprika with coriander, allspice, fenugreek and ginger.
4. Let them cook for 22 min. Stir in the soy sauce with a pinch of salt and pepper.
5. Serve your lentils and potato stew warm with some bread.
6. Enjoy.

NAIROBI
Chicken Roast

Prep Time: 35 mins
Total Time: 42 mins

Servings per Recipe: 4
Calories	387.9
Fat	30.5g
Cholesterol	75.5mg
Sodium	725.3mg
Carbohydrates	2.6g
Protein	25.8g

Ingredients

1/2 C. extra virgin olive oil
1/4 C. chopped scallion
1/4 C. chopped parsley
1/4 C. chopped fresh cilantro
1 tbsp minced garlic
2 tsp paprika
2 tsp ground cumin

1 tsp salt
1/4 tsp turmeric
1/4 tsp cayenne pepper
4 boneless skinless chicken breasts

Directions

1. Get a food blender: Place in it the oil, scallions, parsley, cilantro, garlic, paprika, cumin, salt, turmeric and cayenne pepper.
2. Blend them smooth. Coat the chicken breasts with the mixture. Let them sit for 40 min.
3. Before you do anything else, preheat the grill and grease it.
4. Place the chicken breasts over the grill. Cook them for 6 to 8 min on each side.
5. Serve your roasted chicken breasts warm with some saffron rice or bread.
6. Enjoy.

African
Sweet Honey and Apricot Crock Pot

Prep Time: 30 mins

Total Time: 3 hrs 30 mins

Servings per Recipe: 6

Calories	488.7
Fat	7.9g
Cholesterol	76.7mg
Sodium	645.0mg
Carbohydrates	71.7g
Protein	35.9g

Ingredients

6 large boneless skinless chicken breasts, chopped into chunks
1 tbsp flour
2 large onions, chopped
3 - 4 garlic cloves, chopped
1 - 2 tbsp extra virgin olive oil
1 inch fresh gingerroot, chopped
6 oz. dried apricots
2 tbsp tomato paste
2 (14 oz.) cans chopped tomatoes
2 (14 oz.) cans chickpeas
3 tbsp honey
1/2 pint chicken stock

1 pinch saffron
4 tsp ras el hanout spice mix
1 tsp ground coriander
1 tsp ground cinnamon
1 tsp ground cumin
1 tsp cayenne pepper
salt and black pepper
chopped fresh coriander
2 carrots, peeled & diced
1 preserved lemon, wedges
harissa

Directions

1. Place a pan over medium heat. Heat in it the oil. Cook in it the garlic with onion for 6 to 8 min.
2. Stir in the chicken stock. Add the flour gradually while mixing them all the time. Stir in the tomato paste with honey, herbs, ginger, spices, a pinch of salt and pepper.
3. Mix in the tomato and stir them well. Pour the mixture into a slow cooker. Stir in the dry apricots and put on the lid. Let them cook for 3 h 30 min to 4 h 30 min on high or 9 h on low.
4. Once the time is up, serve your chicken stew hot with some couscous, rice, or bread. Enjoy.

YELLOW
Peanut Stew from Senegal

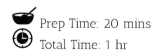 Prep Time: 20 mins

Total Time: 1 hr

Servings per Recipe: 4

Calories	1036.6
Fat	73.6g
Cholesterol	112.2mg
Sodium	1126.2mg
Carbohydrates	42.8g
Protein	61.9g

Ingredients

1 large onion, chopped
2 garlic cloves, minced
1/4 tsp cayenne
2 tbsp vegetable oil
1/4 C. curry powder
1 tbsp yellow curry paste
1 quart chicken stock
1 quart diced tomatoes with juice

4 C. cooked chicken, diced
3/4 tsp sambal oelek chili paste
1 C. chunky peanut butter
1 (14 oz.) cans coconut milk
1 bunch cilantro, chopped
lemon juice

Directions

1. Place a soup pot over medium heat. Heat in it the oil. Cook in it the onion, garlic and cayenne for 3 min.
2. Add the curry powder with curry paste. Cook them for 2 min.
3. Stir in the chicken stock with tomatoes. Cook them until they start boiling.
4. Lower the heat and let them cook for an extra 16 min. Stir in the chicken with sambal.
5. Let them cook for an extra 12 min. Add the peanut butter with coconut milk. Mix them well.
6. Serve your soup warm. Add to it more flavor by adding some cilantro and lemon juice.
7. Enjoy.

Tangier
Chicken Stew

🥣 Prep Time: 20 mins

🕐 Total Time: 55 mins

Servings per Recipe: 4	
Calories	493.3
Fat	4.6g
Cholesterol	34.0mg
Sodium	1616.6mg
Carbohydrates	92.0g
Protein	27.2g

Ingredients

2 C. chicken broth
1/4 C. tomato paste
2 tbsp of granulated sugar
1 tsp ground cumin
1 tsp salt
1/4 tsp ground red pepper
1/8 tsp ground cinnamon
1/2 C. raisins
1 medium onion, sliced

1 tbsp minced fresh garlic
2 lbs. butternut squash, peeled, seeded, and cut into chunks
2 C. frozen green peas
1 (16 oz.) cans chickpeas, drained and rinsed
4 skinless chicken thighs, skin and visible fat removed

Directions

1. Place a stew pot over medium heat. Combine in it the chicken broth, tomato paste, cumin, salt, red pepper, sugar and cinnamon. Mix them well.
2. Add the raisins, onion, garlic, squash, peas, chick-peas, and chicken. Cook them until they start boiling.
3. Lower the heat and put on the lid. Let the stew cook for 26 to 32 min until the veggies become soft.
4. Serve your chicken stew warm with some bread or couscous.
5. Enjoy.

CONGO
Lime Cake

Prep Time: 15 mins
Total Time: 40 mins

Servings per Recipe: 12	
Calories	155.8
Fat	3.3g
Cholesterol	37.3mg
Sodium	101.5mg
Carbohydrates	29.1g
Protein	2.7g

Ingredients

1 C. sugar
2 1/2 tbsp butter
2 eggs
1 lime, juice
1 1/2 C. flour

2 1/4 tsp baking powder
chopped peanuts

Directions

1. Before you do anything, preheat the oven to 350 F. Grease a baking pan with some butter
2. Get a mixing bowl: Beat in it the butter with sugar until it becomes creamy.
3. Add the eggs with lime juice, flour, baking powder and a pinch of salt. Mix them well.
4. Pour the batter into the greased pan. Place it in the oven and let it cook for 26 min.
5. Allow the cake to cool down completely. Garnish it with some chopped peanuts.
6. Serve your cake with some ice cream.
7. Enjoy.

Ginger and Garlic Prawns

Prep Time: 5 mins
Total Time: 15 mins

Servings per Recipe: 4

Calories	219.1
Fat	12.0g
Cholesterol	214.8mg
Sodium	1040.0mg
Carbohydrates	3.1g
Protein	23.5g

Ingredients

3 tbsp olive oil
3 garlic cloves, crushed
1 tsp paprika
1 tsp ground cumin
1 tsp ginger, fresh grated

1 1/2 lbs. large shrimp, raw & shelled
1/8 tsp sea salt
2 tbsp fresh coriander, chopped

Directions

1. Place a pan over medium heat. Heat in it the oil. Cook in it the garlic for 3 to 4 min.
2. Stir in the ginger, paprika, and cumin. Cook them for 1 min.
3. Add the prawns, salt and cilantro. Cook them for 6 min.
4. Serve your spicy prawns warm with some rice.
5. Enjoy.

KOSHARI
(North African Rice and Bean Casserole)

Prep Time: 10 mins
Total Time: 45 mins

Servings per Recipe: 6
Calories	391.0
Fat	9.9g
Cholesterol	0.0mg
Sodium	1183.4mg
Carbohydrates	67.6g
Protein	10.3g

Ingredients

2 tbsp oil
1 1/4 C. lentils
3 C. boiling water
1 tsp salt
1 dash pepper
1 1/2 C. rice
1 C. boiling water
3/4 C. tomato paste
3 C. tomato juice
1 green pepper, chopped
1/2 C. celery leaves, chopped

1 tbsp sugar
1/2 tsp salt
1 tsp cumin
1/4 tsp cayenne pepper
2 tbsp oil
3 onions, sliced
4 garlic cloves, minced

Directions

1. To make the lentils and rice:
2. Place a large saucepan over medium heat. Heat in it 2 tbsp of oil. Cook in it the lentils for 6 min.
3. Stir in 3 C. of hot stock with a pinch of salt and pepper. Let them cook for 11 min.
4. Add the rice with 1 C. of stock. Cook them until they start boiling.
5. Lower the heat and put on the lid. let them cook for 26 min.
6. To make the sauce:
7. Place a large saucepan over medium heat.
8. Stir in it the tomato sauce with tomato juice, green pepper, celery leaves, sugar, cumin, cayenne pepper, and salt.
9. Cook them until they start boiling. Lower the heat and let them cook for 25 to 32 min.
10. To make the onion:
11. Place a small pan over medium heat. Heat in it the oil.

12. Cook in it the onion with garlic for 4 to 6 min until it becomes brown.
13. Divide the rice and lentils mix on serving plates. Drizzle over them the tomato sauce followed by the browned onion.
14. Serve your koshari warm.
15. Enjoy.

CHICKEN
Kabobs Ojini

Prep Time: 12 hrs
Total Time: 12 hrs 10 mins

Servings per Recipe: 4

Calories	169.5
Fat	5.7g
Cholesterol	80.0mg
Sodium	437.4mg
Carbohydrates	1.3g
Protein	26.8g

Ingredients

Kabobs
17.5 boneless skinless chicken breasts, diced
8 pre-soaked wooden skewers
4 metal skewers
Marinade
1/2 tsp coriander seed, ground
1/2 tsp cumin seed, ground
1/2 tsp fennel seed, ground
1 - 2 tsp sweet smoked paprika
2 garlic cloves, peeled and crushed

1/2 tsp salt
1 pinch saffron
2 tbsp boiling water
1 tbsp chopped fresh oregano
1 bay leaf, crumbled
2 tsp sherry wine vinegar
2 tsp olive oil
Topping
chopped flat leaf parsley

Directions

1. Get a mixing bowl: Mix in it all the marinade ingredients. Add the chicken dices and toss them to coat.
2. Cover the bowl with a plastic wrap and let it sit for at least 3 h or an overnight.
3. Before you do anything, preheat the grill and grease it.
4. Drain the chicken dices and thread them into skewers. Place them on the grill and cook them for 6 to 7 min.
5. Serve your kabobs warm with some bread, a salad and your favorite dressing.
6. Enjoy.

African Mashed Potato Lunch Box

Prep Time: 15 mins
Total Time: 1 hr 15 mins

Servings per Recipe: 4
Calories	195.6
Fat	4.6g
Cholesterol	11.6mg
Sodium	930.6mg
Carbohydrates	35.0g
Protein	4.6g

Ingredients

4 garlic cloves
1/2 tsp extra virgin olive oil
2 medium sweet potatoes
2 medium russet potatoes
1 tbsp unsalted butter
2 tbsp chopped fresh parsley
1 tbsp fresh sage, chopped

1 1/2 tsp salt
1 pinch black pepper
1/2 C. plain yogurt
1 sprig fresh parsley

Directions

1. Before you do anything, preheat the oven to 400 F.
2. Lay the garlic in a small piece of foil. Pour over it the oil then wrap the foil around it.
3. Place the garlic on a baking tray with the potatoes. Pierce the potatoes several times with a fork.
4. Place the tray baking tray in the oven on the lower rack. Cook them for 22 min. Flip the potatoes and let them cook for an extra 25 min.
5. Remove the sweet potatoes with garlic from the tray. Place the russet potato back in the oven.
6. Let it cook for an extra 14 min. Turn off the oven and let them cool down for a while.
7. Discard the potatoes peel and place them in a large mixing bowl.
8. Squeeze the garlic and add it to the bowl. Use a potato masher to mash the potatoes until they become smooth.
9. Add the remaining ingredients and mix them well.
10. Adjust the seasoning of your mashed potato then serve it with some roasted meat.
11. Enjoy.

BLACK COUSCOUS
Salad

Prep Time: 20 mins
Total Time: 2 hrs 50 mins

Servings per Recipe: 8

Calories	129.5
Fat	5.7g
Cholesterol	20.0mg
Sodium	437.4mg
Carbohydrates	1.3g
Protein	23.8g

Ingredients

1 C. uncooked couscous
1 1/4 C. chicken broth
1/4 C. extra virgin olive oil
1/4 C. fresh lime juice
1 tbsp red wine vinegar
2 tsp cumin
1 red pepper, seeded and chopped
1/3 C. cilantro
2 tbsp garlic, crushed
8 green onions, chopped

1 (16 oz.) cans black beans, rinsed and drained
1 - 2 tomatoes, diced
1 jalapeno, seed and diced
1 C. feta cheese
1 C. frozen whole kernel corn
salt and pepper

Directions

1. Place a large saucepan over medium heat. Heat in it the broth until it starts boiling.
2. Add the couscous. Put on the lid and turn off the heat. Let it sit for 6 min.
3. Get a mixing bowl: Mix in it the olive oil, lime juice, vinegar and cumin.
4. Stir in the green onions, red pepper, cilantro, corn, optional tomatoes and beans.
5. Use a fork to stir the couscous. Add it to the veggies salad and toss them to coat.
6. Adjust the seasoning of your salad then serve it.
7. Enjoy.

Semolina Cake
with Lemon Syrup

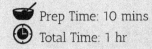 Prep Time: 10 mins

Total Time: 1 hr

Servings per Recipe: 12
Calories	327.1
Fat	12.0g
Cholesterol	31.5mg
Sodium	377.3mg
Carbohydrates	51.0g
Protein	4.5g

Ingredients

3/4 C. butter, melted
3/4 C. sugar
1 1/4 C. buttermilk
2 C. semolina
1 1/2 tsp vanilla
1 tbsp baking powder
1 1/2 tsp baking soda

Glaze
1 C. sugar
1 C. water
lemon, juice

Directions

1. Before you do anything, preheat the oven to 350 F. Grease a baking pan.
2. Get a mixing bowl: Mix in it the buttermilk with sugar. Add the
3. Get a mixing bowl: Stir in it the semolina, vanilla, baking powder and baking soda.
4. Add it to the buttermilk mix with the melted butter. Mix them well.
5. Pour the batter into the greased pan. Place it in the oven and let it cook for 26 min.
6. Once the time is up, place the cake aside and let it sit for 22 min.
7. Place a heavy saucepan over medium heat. Stir in it the syrup ingredients.
8. Cook them until they start boiling. Lower the heat and let them cook for 22 to 26 min.
9. Pour the syrup all over the semolina cake. Allow it to cool down completely.
10. Garnish the cake with some chopped nuts of your choice. Serve it with some tea.
11. Enjoy.

RICE AND BEANS
Africom

Prep Time: 12 mins
Total Time: 42 mins

Servings per Recipe: 12

Calories	230.6
Fat	2.8g
Cholesterol	0.0mg
Sodium	109.7mg
Carbohydrates	44.9g
Protein	5.2g

Ingredients

2 tbsp oil
1 medium onion
3 C. rice
6 C. water
1 (15 oz.) cans kidney beans

1 tbsp smokey paprika
2 bay leaves
salt
pepper

Directions

1. Place a large saucepan over medium heat. Heat in it the oil. Sauté in it the onion for 5 min.
2. Stir in 6 C. of water with paprika, and bay leaves. Season with salt and pepper.
3. Cook them until they start boiling. Add the rice with beans and stir them well.
4. Lower the heat and put on the lid. Let them cook for 26 min. Serve your rice pan warm with tomato sauce.
5. Enjoy.

Rice
Pudding Nakaru

🥣 Prep Time: 10 mins
🕐 Total Time: 35 mins

Servings per Recipe: 6
Calories	398.0
Fat	6.6g
Cholesterol	24.2mg
Sodium	118.4mg
Carbohydrates	73.4g
Protein	10.0g

Ingredients

2 C. short-grain rice
6 C. water
4 1/4 C. milk
1 pinch salt

1/2 vanilla bean
6 tbsp sugar

Directions

1. Before you do anything, preheat the oven to 450 F. Grease a baking sheet and place it aside.
2. Get a mixing bowl:
3. Place a large pan of water over medium heat. Heat it until it starts boiling. Stir in the rice and let it cook for 6 min.
4. Place a heavy saucepan over medium heat. Heat in it the milk until it starts boiling.
5. Drain the rice and add it to milk. Stir in the salt, vanilla bean, and sugar. Put on the lid and let it cook for 16 to 19 min.
6. Serve your rice pudding warm or cold with some chopped nuts.
7. Enjoy.

MOMBASA
Avocado Salad

 Prep Time: 25 mins

Total Time: 25 mins

Servings per Recipe: 4

Calories	416.5
Fat	22.9g
Cholesterol	0.0mg
Sodium	94.8mg
Carbohydrates	49.1g
Protein	5.9g

Ingredients

4 tbsp olive oil
1 small onion, chopped
2 plump garlic cloves, crushed
1 1/8 C. basmati rice
2 C. vegetable stock
1 tomatoes, peeled, seeded and diced
2 large green onions, chopped
2 tbsp chopped parsley

salt and pepper
1/3 C. black olives, pitted
1 small avocado, pitted, peeled and diced

Directions

1. Place a heavy saucepan over medium heat. Heat in it the oil. Cook in it the onion with garlic for 2 min.
2. Stir in the rice and cook them for 2 to 3 min. Stir in the stock and cook them until they start boiling.
3. Add the rice and put on the lid. Let them cook for 13 min until the rice is done.
4. Place a small skillet over medium heat. Heat in it the oil. Sauté in it the tomato, green onions, parsley and salt and pepper for 6 min.
5. Turn off the heat and add the avocado with olives. Add the rice and stir them well with a fork.
6. Serve your warm rice salad right away or let it cool down in fridge for few minutes then serve it cold.
7. Enjoy.

West African
Peanut Soup

Prep Time: 10 mins
Total Time: 25 mins

Servings per Recipe: 4
Calories	184.7
Fat	9.1g
Cholesterol	0.0mg
Sodium	259.6mg
Carbohydrates	20.0g
Protein	11.9g

Ingredients

2 medium onions, sliced
2 large tomatoes, peeled
2 lbs. spinach, trimmed and chopped
4 tbsp peanut butter

salt
pepper
oil

Directions

1. Get a small mixing bowl: Whisk in it the peanut butter with a splash of hot water until it becomes thin.
2. Place a large saucepan over medium heat. Heat in it the oil. Cook in it the onion for 3 min.
3. Stir in the tomato with spinach, a pinch of salt and pepper. Put on the lid and cook them for 6 min over low heat.
4. Add the peanut butter mix. Cook them for 6 to 11 min until the veggies are done while adding more water if needed.
5. Serve your spinach stew warm with some rice, couscous or mashed potato.
6. Enjoy.

CHICKPEA
Rice Casserole

Prep Time: 10 mins
Total Time: 40 mins

Servings per Recipe: 6

Calories	368.6
Fat	7.2g
Cholesterol	0.0mg
Sodium	426.8mg
Carbohydrates	67.1g
Protein	9.0g

Ingredients

1 medium onion, chopped
2 garlic cloves, minced
2 tbsp olive oil
2 C. long grain brown rice, cooked
1 (16 oz.) cans chickpeas, drained
1/2 C. water
2 tbsp parsley, chopped
1/2 tsp salt

1/2 tsp dried basil
1/2 tsp dried marjoram
1/2 tsp ground cumin
1/4 tsp ground turmeric
1/4 tsp fresh ground pepper

Directions

1. Place a pan over medium heat. Heat in it the oil. Cook in it the garlic with onion for 3 min.
2. Add the remaining ingredients. Put on the lid and let them cook for 16 to 22 min over low heat.
3. Serve your rice casserole warm with some leftover chicken or meat.
4. Enjoy.

Cape
Custard Pie

🥣 Prep Time: 20 mins
🕐 Total Time: 35 mins

Servings per Recipe: 1
Calories	1263.1
Fat	69.7g
Cholesterol	432.9mg
Sodium	715.1mg
Carbohydrates	125.9g
Protein	33.9g

Ingredients

1/2 lb. puff pastry
1 1/2 tsp butter
1 pinch salt
1 cinnamon stick
3 C. milk
2 tsp custard powder
3 tsp corn flour

3 tsp cake flour
2 tbsp cold milk
1/2 C. sugar
4 large eggs, separated
1/2 tsp almond essence
cinnamon-sugar mixture

Directions

1. Before you do anything, preheat the oven to 400 F. Grease a baking sheet and place it aside.
2. Get a mixing bowl: Heat in it the milk until it starts boiling. Stir in the butter with the cinnamon stick and a pinch of salt.
3. Lower the heat and let it simmer.
4. Get a mixing bowl: Stir in it the custard powder, corn flour and cake flour. Add the cold milk and combine them well.
5. Add some of the hot milk to bowl and mix them until the batter becomes smooth.
6. Add it to the saucepan with the remaining hot milk. Mix them well.
7. Stir in 4 tbsp of sugar then cook them until they start boiling while stirring them all the time until it becomes slightly thick to make the custard.
8. Turn off the heat and discard the cinnamon stick.
9. Get a large mixing bowl: beat in it the egg white until they become stiff. Add the remaining sugar and beat until their soft peaks.
10. Get a mixing bowl: Beat in it the egg yolks until they become pale. Add the custard gradually while mixing all the time.
11. Gold the almond extract followed by the egg white into the batter.

12. Grease 2 pie dishes with some butter. Cover them completely with the puff pastry.
13. Pour the custard in the pans then place them in the oven and let them cook for 11 to 16 min in the oven.
14. Allow the pies to cool down completely. Serve them with your favorite toppings.
15. Enjoy.

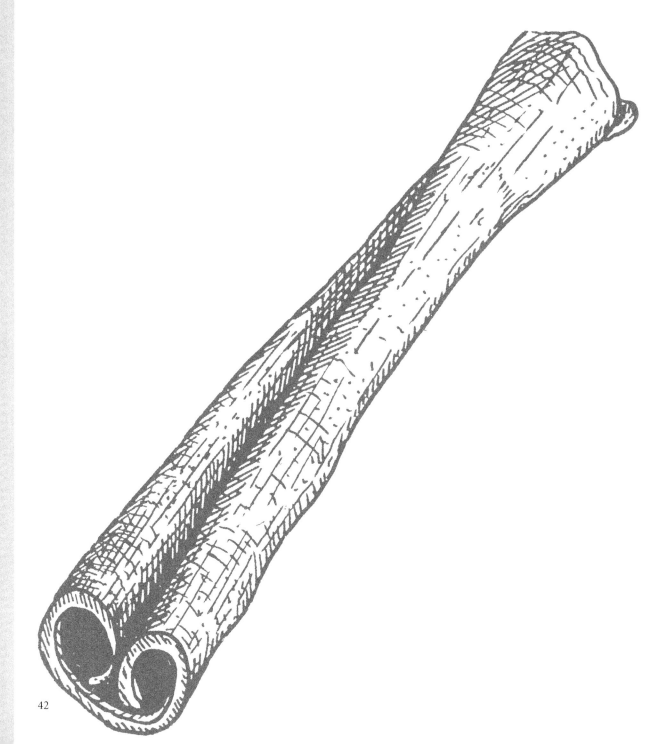

Ife's
Steak Sauce

Prep Time: 5 mins
Total Time: 35 mins

Servings per Recipe: 8
Calories	116.2
Fat	3.6g
Cholesterol	0.0mg
Sodium	511.9mg
Carbohydrates	21.4g
Protein	1.1g

Ingredients

2 tbsp oil
1 large onion, diced
2 cloves garlic, chopped
1/2 C. water
2 large tomatoes, diced
1 C. ketchup
1/2 C. Worcestershire sauce

3/4 C. fruit chutney, see appendix
1/4 C. brown sugar
2 tbsp vinegar
1 tsp Tabasco sauce

Directions

1. Place a pan over medium heat. Heat in it the oil. Cook in it the onion with garlic for 3 min.
2. Stir in the rest of the ingredients. Let it cook for 32 min over low heat.
3. Serve your sauce warm with your favorite sauce.
4. Enjoy.

COUSCOUS
Masala

Prep Time: 10 mins
Total Time: 30 mins

Servings per Recipe: 4

Calories	274.4
Fat	10.4g
Cholesterol	0.0mg
Sodium	249.0mg
Carbohydrates	37.1g
Protein	7.9g

Ingredients

2 tbsp pine nuts, toasted
2 tbsp olive oil
1 shallot, peeled and minced
1 carrot, peeled and shredded
2 tbsp lemon juice

1 tbsp garam masala
1 1/4 C. chicken broth
1 C. Israeli couscous

Directions

1. Place a large heavy saucepan over medium heat. Heat in it the oil. Cook in it the carrot with shallot for 2 min.

2. Add the lemon juice with garam masala and broth. Cook them until they start boiling to make the sauce.

3. Add the couscous. Lower the heat and put on the lid. Let them cook for 9 to 11 min.

4. Once the time is up, turn off the heat. Let the couscous sit for 6 min then stir it with a fork.

5. Get a serving bowl: Stir in it the couscous with the sauce and pinenuts.

6. Garnish it with some parsley or green onion then serve it.

7. Enjoy.

Classic Egyptian
Macaroni Casserole with Béchamel Sauce

Prep Time: 30 mins
Total Time: 1 hr 20 mins

Servings per Recipe: 4

Calories	1485.9
Fat	75.3g
Cholesterol	407.8mg
Sodium	899.7mg
Carbohydrates	129.2g
Protein	74.0g

Ingredients

1 (16 oz.) boxes penne pasta
2 lbs. ground beef
1 medium onion, chopped
2 garlic cloves, minced
2 tbsp chopped fresh parsley
1 tbsp fresh thyme
1 tsp cinnamon
1 (8 oz.) cans tomato sauce
1 beaten egg
1 dash parmesan cheese
8 C. cold milk

6 tbsp butter
6 tbsp flour
1 tsp fresh thyme
1/2 tsp nutmeg
2 beaten eggs
salt
white pepper
black pepper

Directions

1. Before you do anything, preheat the oven to 400 F.
2. To make the paste:
3. Cook the pasta by following the instructions on the package.
4. To make the meat sauce:
5. Place a small pan over medium heat. Heat in it the oil. Cook in it the garlic with onion for 3 min.
6. Stir in the beef and cook them for 7 min. Discard the excess fat. Mix in the parsley, thyme, and cinnamon.
7. Add the tomato sauce then let them cook for 11 min over low heat. Turn off the heat and let the sauce cool down for a while.
8. To make the béchamel sauce:
9. Place a large saucepan over medium heat. Heat in it the butter until it melts. Add the flour and mix them well.

10. Cook it for 2 to 3 min until it becomes golden while mixing it all the time.
11. Add to them the boiling milk gradually while mixing them all the time with a whisk.
12. Stir in the nutmeg and thyme.
13. Get a large mixing bowl: Stir in it the half of the béchamel sauce with the pasta, a pinch of salt and pepper.
14. Pour half of the pasta in a casserole dish. Cover it by half of the meat sauce.
15. Pour the remaining pasta on top followed by the remaining tomato sauce.
16. Cover them with the remaining béchamel sauce and some cheese of your choice.
17. Place the pasta casserole in the oven and let it cook for 46 to 61 min.
18. Allow the pasta casserole to sit for few minutes then serve it warm.
19. Enjoy.

African
Breakfast Eggs

🥣 Prep Time: 10 mins
🕐 Total Time: 25 mins

Servings per Recipe: 2
Calories	442.7
Fat	27.9g
Cholesterol	590.0mg
Sodium	1461.7mg
Carbohydrates	26.3g
Protein	21.2g

Ingredients

2 tbsp butter
2 onions, chopped
2 1/2 tsp hot curry powder
2 tbsp cake flour
1 tsp salt
fresh ground black pepper
1 tbsp sugar

1 tbsp apple cider vinegar
1 1/2 C. water
6 hard-boiled eggs, shelled and halved

Directions

1. Place a saucepan over medium heat. Heat in it the butter. Cook in it the onion for 5 min. Turn off the heat.
2. Get a mixing bowl: Stir in it the curry powder, flour, salt, pepper, sugar and vinegar.
3. Stir the mixture into the cooked onion with water. Let them cook for 12 to 16 min to make the curry sauce.
4. Place hard boiled eggs on a serving plate. Pour the curry sauce all over them.
5. Garnish them with some parsley then serve them right away.
6. Enjoy.

TUNISIAN
Hot Pot

Prep Time: 10 mins
Total Time: 36 mins

Servings per Recipe: 4
Calories	235.0
Fat	2.0g
Cholesterol	0.0mg
Sodium	401.0mg
Carbohydrates	49.1g
Protein	9.1g

Ingredients

1 sliced onion
1/4 C. vegetable stock
3 C. sliced cabbage
1 dash salt
1 large green pepper, diced
1 (28 oz.) cans diced tomatoes, undrained
1 (16 oz.) cans chickpeas

1/4 C. raisins
2 tsp ground coriander
1/2 tsp turmeric
1/4 tsp cinnamon
1 tbsp lemon juice
salt

Directions

1. Place a large saucepan over medium heat. Heat in it the oil. Cook in it the onion for 6 min.
2. Stir in the cabbage with a pinch of salt. Cook them for 6 min.
3. Stir in the pepper with spices then cook them for 1 min
4. Add the tomatoes with raisins stock, and chickpeas. Put on the lid and let them cook for 16 min over low heat.
5. Once the time is up, stir in the lemon juice. Adjust the seasoning of your stew then serve it warm and enjoy.
6. Enjoy.

Herbed
Congo Carrots

Prep Time: 5 mins
Total Time: 17 mins

Servings per Recipe: 4
Calories	175.8
Fat	11.8g
Cholesterol	30.5mg
Sodium	179.7mg
Carbohydrates	17.8g
Protein	1.4g

Ingredients

1 lb. carrot, cut into sticks
1/4 C. butter
1 tbsp sugar
1/2 inch piece ginger, shredded
1 orange, grated rind

salt and pepper
2 - 4 sprigs dill, chopped

Directions

1. Place a heavy saucepan over medium heat. Stir in it the carrots with butter, ginger, sugar, a pinch of salt and pepper.
2. Cook them until they start boiling. Lower the heat and let them cook for 13 min until the carrots soften.
3. Serve your carrots warm or cold with some bread or as a topping.
4. Garnish them with some fresh dill sprigs.
5. Enjoy.

TRADITIONAL
Moroccan Chicken Tagine with Olives

Prep Time: 30 mins
Total Time: 1 hr 10 mins

Servings per Recipe: 4
Calories	221.0
Fat	13.8g
Cholesterol	68.0mg
Sodium	1124.3mg
Carbohydrates	8.3g
Protein	17.7g

Ingredients

8 skinless chicken thighs
3/4 C. onion, chopped
1/2 C. fresh cilantro, chopped
1/2 C. Italian parsley, chopped
2 garlic cloves, minced
1 tsp ground cumin
1 tsp ground ginger
1 tsp sweet paprika

1/2 tsp black pepper
1/4 tsp saffron, crushed
2 C. green olives, pitted
1/2 preserved lemon, chopped
1 lemon, juice
salt
black pepper

Directions

1. Place a tagine or a stew pot over medium heat.
2. Heat in it a splash of oil. Brown in it the chicken thighs for 2 to 3 min on each side.
3. Add the onion, cilantro, parsley, garlic, cumin, ginger, paprika, ½ tsp of the pepper, and saffron.
4. Cook them for 2 min while stirring them often. Pour 2 C. of water over them.
5. Put on the lid and let them over low high heat until they start boiling.
6. Once the time is up, stir in the olives with lemon juice, preserved lemon, and a pinch of salt.
7. Put on the lid and let the stew cook for 22 min.
8. Serve your stew warm with some bread.
9. Enjoy.

Vegetarian
Tanzanian Skillet

🥣 Prep Time: 10 mins
🕐 Total Time: 45 mins

Servings per Recipe: 4
Calories	361.2
Fat	29.1g
Cholesterol	24.5mg
Sodium	849.7mg
Carbohydrates	21.0g
Protein	11.8g

Ingredients

2 lbs. spinach, chopped
1 1/2 oz. peanut butter
1 tomatoes, peeled and chopped
1 onion, chopped
2 tsp curry powder

1 C. coconut milk
3 tbsp ghee
1 tsp salt

Directions

1. Get a mixing bowl: Whisk in it the peanut butter with coconut milk.
2. Place a large skillet over medium heat. Heat in it the ghee. Cook in it the tomato with onion, curry powder and a pinch of salt for 6 min.
3. Stir in the spinach and cook them for 16 to 21 min over low heat.
4. Once the time is up, stir in the peanut butter and milk mix. Let them cook for an extra 6 min.
5. Serve your peanut butter and spinach stew warm with some rice.
6. Enjoy.

UGANDAN
Potato Curry with Piri Piri Sauce

🥘 Prep Time: 5 mins
🕐 Total Time: 20 mins

Servings per Recipe: 4
Calories	271.3
Fat	7.1g
Cholesterol	0.0mg
Sodium	26.7mg
Carbohydrates	48.1g
Protein	5.5g

Ingredients

2 1/4 lb. potato, peeled & parboiled, cooked
1 medium onion, peeled & chopped
2 garlic cloves, minced
1/2 tsp turmeric
1/2 tsp piri piri chili sauce
1/2 tsp ground cinnamon
1/2 tsp ground coriander

1 tsp tomato puree
1 tbsp lemon juice
1 tbsp fresh parsley, chopped
salt
2 tbsp cooking oil

Directions

1. Place a stew pot over medium heat. Heat in it the oil. Cook in it the onion for 3 min.
2. Stir in the garlic and cook them for 1 min. Stir in the chili sauce with turmeric, cinnamon, coriander, and a pinch of salt.
3. Cook them for an extra minute. Stir in the tomato puree, lemon juice, and parsley.
4. Add the diced potato with 3/4 C. of water. Let the potato stew cook for 10 to 12 min or until the potato soften.
5. Serve your potato curry warm with some bread or white rice.
6. Enjoy.

Coconut
and Corn Curry

Prep Time: 20 mins
Total Time: 35 mins

Servings per Recipe: 6
Calories	276.5
Fat	12.5g
Cholesterol	5.0mg
Sodium	64.3mg
Carbohydrates	42.3g
Protein	6.4g

Ingredients

1 tbsp butter
1 medium onion, chopped
1 garlic clove, minced
1/2 tsp curry powder
5 C. corn, cut from cob
1/2 tsp cornstarch
1 C. coconut milk
2 medium tomatoes, peeled, seeded, and

chopped
salt
pepper, ground

Directions

1. Place a large saucepan over medium heat. Melt in it the butter.
2. Cook in it the garlic with onion for 3 min. Stir in the curry powder and cook them for 30 sec.
3. Get a mixing bowl: Mix in it the cornstarch with coconut milk.
4. Stir into the onion with corn, tomato, a pinch of salt and pepper. Let them cook for 8 min.
5. Serve your corn curry warm with some rice and leftover roasted meat.
6. Enjoy.

BEEF SOUP
Himba

Prep Time: 10 mins
Total Time: 1 hr 50 mins

Servings per Recipe: 4

Calories	586.8
Fat	36.2g
Cholesterol	134.0mg
Sodium	1859.0mg
Carbohydrates	29.0g
Protein	35.6g

Ingredients

1 lb. beef stew meat, cubed
2 tbsp flour
2 onions, chopped
2 tbsp butter
4 C. beef broth
2 tbsp curry powder

2 bay leaves
2 potatoes, sliced
2 tbsp distilled white vinegar
2 tsp salt

Directions

1. Get a mixing bowl: Mix in it the beef with onion, flour and a pinch of salt.
2. Place a large stew pot over medium heat. Melt in it the butter. Add to it the beef and onion mix.
3. Cook them for 2 to 3 min while stirring them often. Stir in the broth, curry powder, and bay leaves.
4. Put on the lid and let them cook for 32 min over low heat.
5. Stir in the potatoes, vinegar, and salt. Put on the lid and let the stew cook for an extra 62 min over low heat.
6. Serve your beef curry warm with some bread or rice.
7. Enjoy.

West African
Samosas

🥣 Prep Time: 20 mins
🕐 Total Time: 55 mins

Servings per Recipe: 8
Calories	327.9
Fat	19.2g
Cholesterol	23.2mg
Sodium	252.5mg
Carbohydrates	34.9g
Protein	5.3g

Ingredients

2 Idaho potatoes, peeled and diced
salt
1 tbsp extra virgin olive oil
1 small onion, chopped
1/2 jalapeno pepper, seeds and stem removed, chopped
1/2 inch fresh gingerroot, peeled, grated
1 garlic clove, chopped
1 tsp ground coriander
2 tsp curry powder
1 tsp ground cumin
1/2 tsp ground allspice
1/8 tsp cinnamon
black pepper
1 roma tomato, seeded, chopped
1/4 C. frozen peas

1/4-1/2 C. vegetable stock
flour, for rolling dough
2 nine inch rounds refrigerated ready-made pie dough
1 egg, beaten with a splash of water
Cilantro Aioli
1 bunch fresh mint leaves
1 bunch fresh cilantro leaves
1 jalapeno pepper, seeds and stem removed
1 tsp sugar
2 limes, juice
1 tbsp extra virgin olive oil
1 garlic clove, grated
1 inch fresh gingerroot, grated

Directions

1. To make the samosas:
2. Before you do anything, preheat the oven to 400 F. Line up a baking sheet with parchment paper.
3. Place a large saucepan of water over medium heat. Bring it to a boil. Cook in it the potato for 6 min.
4. Drain the potato and place it aside.
5. Place a large pan over medium heat. Heat in it the oil. Cook in it the onion for 6 min.
6. Stir in the jalapeno, ginger, garlic, coriander, curry powder, cumin, allspice, cinnamon, and salt and pepper.

7. Cook them for 4 min while stirring them often. Add the potatoes, tomato, and peas.

8. Let them cook for an extra 2 min. Stir in the stock then turn off the heat.

9. Place the filling aside to cool down for a while.

10. Spread the pie dough on a floured surface. Slice into 8 wedges. Brush their edges with some egg wash.

11. Place 1 tbsp of the filling in the middle of each wedge. Pull the 3 dough edges on top of the filling and pinch them to seal them.

12. Place the pierogis on the lined up baking sheet. Brush them again with egg wash then cook them in the oven for 16 to 21 min.

13. To make the mint sauce:

14. Get a blender: Place in it the mint, cilantro, jalapeno, sugar, salt, lime juice, 1 tbsp of water, oil, ginger, garlic and a pinch of salt.

15. Blend them smooth. Pour the sauce into a serving bowl.

16. Serve your pierogis cold or warm with the mint sauce.

17. Enjoy.

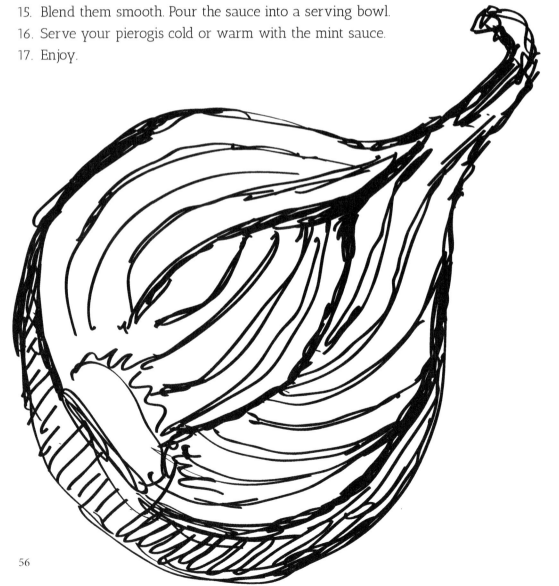

Yoruba
Grilled Vegetable Salad

Prep Time: 10 mins
Total Time: 20 mins

Servings per Recipe: 4
Calories	113.4
Fat	10.5g
Cholesterol	0.0mg
Sodium	11.0mg
Carbohydrates	4.5g
Protein	1.5g

Ingredients

1 lb. zucchini, scrubbed and trimmed
3 tbsp extra-virgin olive oil
salt & freshly ground black pepper
12 large fresh mint leaves, slivered
2 tbsp fresh Italian parsley, chopped
1 tbsp fresh lemon juice
1 garlic clove, minced

1/2 tsp paprika
1/4 tsp ground cumin
1/4 tsp white pepper

Directions

1. Before you do anything, preheat the grill and grease it.
2. Slice the zucchini into 1/4 inch thick pieces.
3. Coat the zucchini slices with olive oil. Sprinkle over them a pinch of salt and pepper.
4. Lay them on the grill and cook them for 4 to 5 min on each side.
5. Allow the zucchini slices to cool down for few minutes. Slice them into strips.
6. Get a small mixing bowl: Whisk in it the remaining oil with mint, parsley, 1 tbsp lemon juice, garlic, paprika, cumin, 1/4 tsp white pepper and a pinch of salt.
7. Drizzle the dressing over the zucchini strips. Serve your salad warm or cold with some lemon wedges.
8. Enjoy.

HOW TO MAKE
Lamb Chops

Prep Time: 5 mins
Total Time: 25 mins

Servings per Recipe: 4

Calories	69.9
Fat	6.9g
Cholesterol	0.0mg
Sodium	146.5mg
Carbohydrates	2.3g
Protein	0.3g

Ingredients

1/4 tsp grated nutmeg
1 pinch clove
1 tsp ground black pepper
1 tsp white pepper
1 1/2 tsp cinnamon
2 tsp ground cardamom
1 pinch cayenne
1 pinch cumin

1 pinch turmeric
1 pinch sea salt
8 lamb rib chops
2 tbsp olive oil

Directions

1. Get a mixing bowl: Combine in it the cinnamon with white pepper, cardamom, black pepper, cayenne, clove, cumin, turmeric, and salt.
2. Rum the lamb chops with the spice mixture.
3. Place a pan over medium heat. Heat in it the oil. Cook in it the lamb chops for 6 to 12 min on each side.
4. Serve your lamb chops warm with a salad of your choice.
5. Enjoy.

Jungle
Potato Mash

Prep Time: 15 mins
Total Time: 40 mins

Servings per Recipe: 4

Calories	85.3
Fat	0.3g
Cholesterol	0.0mg
Sodium	300.9mg
Carbohydrates	19.4g
Protein	3.2g

Ingredients

14 oz. green beans, trimmed
1 potato, medium, peeled and sliced
1 onion, medium, peeled and sliced
1/2 tsp sugar
1/3 tsp white pepper

1/2 tsp salt
1/3 tsp nutmeg
butter

Directions

1. Place a stew pot over medium heat. Lay in it the beans followed by the sliced potato and onion.
2. Pour over them 1/3 C. of water followed by the sugar, pepper and salt.
3. Put on the lid and let them cook until they start boil without stirring them.
4. Once the time is up, lower the heat and let the stew cook for few minutes until the veggies become soft.
5. Drain the veggies then mash them slightly.
6. Get a mixing bowl: Mix in it the mashed veggies with some butter. Serve them warm or cold.
7. Enjoy.

AFRICAN
Meatless Biryani

🥣 Prep Time: 10 mins
🕐 Total Time: 45 mins

Servings per Recipe: 4

Calories	288.7
Fat	3.3g
Cholesterol	7.6mg
Sodium	325.2mg
Carbohydrates	61.5g
Protein	3.9g

Ingredients

1 C. long grain white rice
1/2 tsp salt
1 1/2 tsp ground turmeric
3 tbsp white sugar
1/2 tsp ground cinnamon

1/2 C. dark seedless raisins
1 tbsp butter
2 1/2 C. water

Directions

1. Place a large saucepan over medium heat. Stir in it the rice, salt, turmeric, sugar, cinnamon, raisins, butter and water.
2. Let them cook until they start boiling. Lower the heat and put on the lid. Let them cook for 22 to 32 min or until the rice is done.
3. Once the time is up, stir the rice with a fork.
4. Serve your biryani warm or cold with some chopped nuts.
5. Enjoy.

Spicy Moroccan Cilantro Marinade (Chermoula)

Prep Time: 10 mins
Total Time: 10 mins

Servings per Recipe: 1
Calories   540.6
Fat   55.2g
Cholesterol   0.0mg
Sodium   1188.9mg
Carbohydrates   13.5g
Protein   2.9g

Ingredients

1 bunch fresh cilantro
3 garlic cloves, peeled and bruised
1 tsp cumin, ground
1 tsp coriander, ground
1 tsp paprika, ground

1 small red chili pepper, seeded
1/2 tsp sea salt
1 lemon, juice
1/4 C. olive oil

Directions

1. Get a food processor: Combine in it all the ingredients. Blend them smooth.
2. Pour the marinade in an airtight container. Place it in the fridge until ready to use.
3. You can use this marinade for meat, chicken, veggies or fish.
4. Enjoy.

GARBANZO STEW
Marrakesh

🍲 Prep Time: 20 mins
🕐 Total Time: 1 hr 35 mins

Servings per Recipe: 6
Calories   623.6
Fat   4.9g
Cholesterol   0.0mg
Sodium   371.5mg
Carbohydrates   130.5g
Protein   18.6g

Ingredients

4 C. hot cooked pearl barley
1 tbsp olive oil
1 C. sliced onion
1/2 C. sliced celery
2 cloves garlic, minced
2 carrots, sliced
1 medium zucchini, sliced
1 medium green pepper, seeded and cut into squares
1 C. broccoli floret
1 (15 1/2 oz.) cans garbanzo beans, drained

2 C. vegetable broth
2 tsp soy sauce
2 tsp lemon juice
1/2 tsp ground coriander
1/4 tsp ground ginger
1/8 tsp cayenne pepper
2 tbsp cornstarch, dissolved in 3 tbsp water
chopped cilantro

Directions

1. Get a small mixing bowl: Whisk in it the cornstarch with 3 tbsp of water. Place it aside.
2. Place a pot over medium heat. Heat in it 4 C. of water with barely and 1 tsp of salt.
3. Heat in it until it starts boiling. Lower the heat and let it cook for 46 min until it is done.
4. To make the veggies stew:
5. Place a large saucepan over medium heat. Heat in it the oil.
6. Cook in it the garlic with celery and onion for 4 to 5 min. Stir in the veggies with spices. Put on the lid and let the stew cook for 12 to 16 min or until the veggies become soft.
7. Divide the barley while it is warm between serving plates.
8. Spoon over it the veggies stew while it is hot then serve them warm.
9. Enjoy.

5-Ingredient
West African Okra

Prep Time: 5 mins
Total Time: 25 mins

Servings per Recipe: 6
Calories	39.9
Fat	0.2g
Cholesterol	0.0mg
Sodium	8.0mg
Carbohydrates	9.0g
Protein	1.8g

Ingredients

1 1/2 C. sweet onions, chopped
2 1/2 C. okra, sliced
3 medium tomatoes, chopped

salt & freshly ground black pepper
hot sauce

Directions

1. Place a stew pot over medium heat. Stir in it all the ingredients. Let them cook over low heat until the okra becomes soft.

2. Serve your okra stew warm with some bread.

3. Enjoy.

MOROCCAN
Pilaf

Prep Time: 15 mins
Total Time: 45 mins

Servings per Recipe: 4

Calories	586.4
Fat	16.6g
Cholesterol	23.3mg
Sodium	746.7mg
Carbohydrates	92.1g
Protein	14.9g

Ingredients

2 C. long grain rice
2 tbsp butter
2 tbsp olive oil
1 onion, chopped
2 garlic cloves, chopped
1 - 2 cinnamon stick
1/2 tsp salt
1/2 tsp ginger
1/2 tsp white pepper
1/2 tsp cumin
1/2 tsp turmeric
1/4 C. fresh cilantro, chopped

1/4 C. peas
1 red bell pepper, chopped
1 carrot, chopped
4 1/2 C. chicken stock
1/4 tsp saffron thread, crushed

Directions

1. Place a large saucepan over high heat. Heat in it the stock until it starts boiling.
2. In the meantime, place a deep skillet over medium heat. Stir in it the rest of the ingredients aside for the saffron. Let them cook for 11 min.
3. Stir the saffron with boiling stock into the rice pan.
4. Let them cook for 5 min. Put on the lid and cook them for 26 min until the rice is done
5. Serve your rice skillet warm with some leftover chicken.
6. Enjoy.

West African Dinner (Jollof Rice with Chicken)

Prep Time: 2 hrs
Total Time: 2 hrs

Servings per Recipe: 6
Calories	479.2
Fat	25.9g
Cholesterol	103.5mg
Sodium	556.7mg
Carbohydrates	29.9g
Protein	29.7g

Ingredients

3 lbs. chicken pieces
2 tbsp oil
1 medium onion, chopped
16 ounces canned tomatoes, cut up
1 1/4 C. chicken broth
1 bay leaf
1/2 tsp ground ginger
1/2 tsp cinnamon

1/2 tsp thyme, crushed
1/2 tsp salt
1/4 tsp ground red pepper
1 C. long grain rice
1 tbsp parsley, chopped

Directions

1. Place a pan over medium heat. Heat in it the oil. Cook in it the chicken pieces for 6 to 7 min on each side.
2. Drain the chicken pieces and place them aside.
3. Stir the onion into the remaining oil in the skillet. Cook it for 4 min. Drain it the onion and discard the remaining oil.
4. Stir the chicken back with onion into skillet with undrained tomatoes, broth, and seasonings.
5. Let them cook until they start boiling. Lower the heat and put on the lid. Let the stew cook for 32 min.
6. Discard the fat that rise on top. Stir the rice into the pan. Put on the lid and let them cook for 32 min.
7. Once the time is up, drain the bay lead and discard.
8. Garnish your chicken rice skillet with some parsley then serve it.
9. Enjoy.

GINGER
Lentil Stew

🥣 Prep Time: 10 mins
🕐 Total Time: 45 mins

Servings per Recipe: 6
Calories	344.5
Fat	10.3g
Cholesterol	0.0mg
Sodium	202.3mg
Carbohydrates	46.8g
Protein	17.8g

Ingredients

2 C. orange lentils, rinsed
1/2 tsp salt
1/4 C. vegetable oil
1 large sweet onion, chopped
1 inch piece fresh ginger, grated
3 garlic cloves, crushed
1 tsp coriander powder
1 tsp turmeric

1 tsp cumin seed, crushed
1 tsp cardamom seed, crushed
1/4 tsp ground cinnamon
1/2 tsp cayenne pepper
1 C. fresh tomato, diced peeled

Directions

1. Place a large saucepan over medium heat. Stir in it the lentils with a salt. Cover them with boiling water.
2. Let the lentils cook for 22 min.
3. Once the time is up, drain the lentils. Place it in a mixing bowl and press it with a potato masher to mash it slightly.
4. Place a large skillet over medium heat. Heat in it the oil. Cook in it the onion with garlic for 5 min.
5. Stir in the rest of the ingredients. Cook them for 6 min. Add the lentils and heat them through.
6. Serve your lentils stew warm with some bread.
7. Enjoy.

Sweet Potato Soup

Prep Time: 15 mins
Total Time: 45 mins

Servings per Recipe: 4
Calories	275.4
Fat	6.8g
Cholesterol	0.0mg
Sodium	389.9mg
Carbohydrates	45.9g
Protein	9.7g

Ingredients

1 tsp vegetable oil
1 medium onion, chopped
1 large sweet potato, peeled and diced
2 garlic cloves, minced
4 C. vegetable broth
1 tsp dried thyme
1/2 tsp ground cumin
1 C. chopped tomato

1 - 2 chopped jalapeno
1 (15 1/2 ounce) cans garbanzo beans, drained
1 C. diced zucchini
1/2 C. cooked rice
2 tbsp creamy peanut butter

Directions

1. Place a stew pot over medium heat. Heat in it the oil. Cook in it the onion, sweet potato, and garlic for 3 min.
2. Add the broth, thyme and cumin. Cook them until they start boiling. Put on the lid and lower the heat.
3. Let the stew cook for 16 min. Add the tomatoes, garbanzo beans, jalapenos and zucchini.
4. Put on the lid and let them cook for an extra 16 mins.
5. Add the peanut butter with rice. Heat the soup through then serve it warm.
6. Enjoy.

NIGERIAN
Coconut Cake Pops

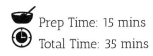 Prep Time: 15 mins
Total Time: 35 mins

Servings per Recipe: 1
Calories   80.3
Fat   4.8g
Cholesterol   35.5mg
Sodium   60.5mg
Carbohydrates   8.4g
Protein   1.3g

Ingredients

1 C. unsweetened flaked coconut
1/4 C. caster sugar
3 egg yolks

1/2 C. self-raising flour

Directions

1. Before you do anything, preheat the oven to 350 F. Line up a baking sheet with parchment paper.
2. Get a mixing bowl: Combine in it the coconut, sugar and egg yolks until you get a soft dough.
3. Shape the dough into a 1 inch size balls. Toss them in the flour and place them on the cookie sheet.
4. Place the cookie sheet in the oven and cook them for 21 min.
5. Allow the cookie to cool down completely then serve them with some tea.
6. Enjoy.

Chicken
Stew Angola

🥣 Prep Time: 10 mins
🕐 Total Time: 55 mins

Servings per Recipe: 4
Calories   861.6
Fat   63.8g
Cholesterol   187.1mg
Sodium   1254.9mg
Carbohydrates   20.3g
Protein   54.4g

Ingredients

1 (3 1/2 lb.) whole chickens, chopped
1 (6 ounce) cans tomato paste
1 large fresh tomato
1 garlic clove, crushed
1 small onion, diced
1/2 C. chunky peanut butter
2 tbsp palm oil
1 bay leaf

1 tsp thyme
1 tsp salt
1 tsp black pepper
1 hot pepper

Directions

1. Place a large pot over medium heat. Place in it the chicken with a bouquette garnish. Cover it with boiling water.

2. Cook the chicken over low medium heat until the chicken is done. Drain the chicken and shred it. Reserve the chicken stock.

3. Place a large skillet over medium heat. Heat in it the oil. Cook in it the onion, hot pepper and garlic for 3 min.

4. Stir in the tomato with tomato paste, peanut butter and 1/2 C. of the chicken stock.

5. Stir in the shredded chicken and cook them for 4 min. Serve your peanut chicken warm with some rice.

6. Enjoy.

JOHANNESBURG
Street Curry

🥣 Prep Time: 20 mins

🕐 Total Time: 2 hrs 20 mins

Servings per Recipe: 6

Calories	214.0
Fat	1.0g
Cholesterol	0.9mg
Sodium	169.6mg
Carbohydrates	53.0g
Protein	3.7g

Ingredients

3 1/3 lb. boneless lamb shoulder, cut into pieces
oil
4 onions, peeled and chopped
2 - 4 garlic cloves, peeled and minced
1 piece fresh gingerroot, peeled and crushed
1 tbsp cape Malay curry powder
1 tsp ground coriander
1 tsp ground cumin
1/2 tsp turmeric
1/4 tsp salt
black pepper
1 cinnamon stick

3 cloves
2 bay leaves
2 carrots, peeled and diced
9 oz. dried apricots, soaked in warm water and drained
2 bananas, peeled and sliced
2 tbsp tomato paste
3 1/2 tbsp wine vinegar
1 C. meat stock
3 tbsp apricot jam
3 tbsp natural yoghurt

Directions

1. Place a large saucepan over medium heat. Heat in it the oil. Cook in it the garlic with onion for 3 min.
2. Stir in the ginger with all the spices. Cook them for 1 to 2 min.
3. Add the lamb pieces then cook them for 3 min on each side.
4. Stir in the vinegar with stock, carrots, bay leaves, apricots, tomato paste, cinnamon stick, a pinch of salt and pepper.
5. Put on the lid and let them cook for 1 h 40 min over low heat.
6. Once the time is up, add the apricot jam and the yoghurt. Let the stew cook for 3 to 4 min then serve it warm with some rice.
7. Enjoy.

Peanut Butter
Chicken Pan

🥣 Prep Time: 5 mins
🕐 Total Time: 30 mins

Servings per Recipe: 4
Calories	303.1
Fat	16.3g
Cholesterol	97.2mg
Sodium	154.8mg
Carbohydrates	9.5g
Protein	30.1g

Ingredients

1 tbsp oil
4 chicken thigh fillets, cubed
9 oz. boneless chicken breasts, cubed
1 onion, chopped
2 tsp curry powder
15 oz. tomatoes

2 tbsp peanut butter
1/2 green pepper, sliced
2 tsp chicken stock powder

Directions

1. Place a pan over medium heat. Heat in it the oil. Cook in it the chicken with onion for 6 min.
2. Stir in the curry powder and cook them for 2 min.
3. Stir in the tomato with peanut butter, green pepper, stock powder, a pinch of salt and pepper.
4. Cook them until they start boiling. Put on the lid and let the stew cook for 22 min.
5. Serve your chicken stew warm with some rice.
6. Enjoy.

SUDANESE
Tahini Spread

Prep Time: 5 mins
Total Time: 5 mins

Servings per Recipe: 4
Calories   261.4
Fat   19.4g
Cholesterol   0.8mg
Sodium   63.0mg
Carbohydrates   16.2g
Protein   9.7g

Ingredients

2/3 C. tahini
2/3 C. plain nonfat yogurt
3 cloves garlic, minced
2 lemons, juice
2 tbsp chopped fresh parsley

salt
black pepper

Directions

1. Get a food processor: Combine in it the garlic, salt, black pepper, and tahini. Blend them smooth.

2. Mix in the yogurt and lemon juice. Blend them smooth.

3. Pour the dip in a serving bowl. Garnish it with parsley. Serve it with some bread or veggies sticks.

4. Enjoy.

Semolina Cake
with Vanilla Syrup

🥣 Prep Time: 15 mins
🕐 Total Time: 1 hr

Servings per Recipe: 9
Calories   627.9
Fat   22.6g
Cholesterol   99.1mg
Sodium   452.4mg
Carbohydrates   104.8g
Protein   4.9g

Ingredients

Cake
1 C. semolina flour
1 C. yogurt
1 C. sugar
1 C. butter, melted
2 tbsp baking powder
2 beaten eggs

Syrup
3 C. sugar
1 C. water
1 tsp vanilla
1/2 lemons
1 cinnamon stick

Directions

1. To prepare the cake:
2. Before you do anything, preheat the oven to 350 F. Grease a baking pan with some butter Get a mixing bowl: Combine in it the flour, sugar, and baking powder. Mix in the melted butter with yogurt.
3. Add the eggs and combine them well. Use a hand mixer to blend the batter until it becomes smooth. Transfer the batter into the greased pan. Place it in the middle of the oven. Let it cook for 46 min.
4. To prepare the syrup:
5. Place a heavy saucepan over medium heat. Combine in it 3 C. of sugar with 1 C. of water. Stir in the cinnamon stick with vanilla and the juice of half a lemon including the lemon half.
6. Bring the syrup to a rolling boil for 2 min. Turn off the heat.
7. Once the time is up, allow the cake to cool down for 6 min. Pour over it the hot syrup.
8. Let the cake cool down completely. Garnish it with some chopped nuts then serve it with some tea or ice cream.
9. Enjoy.

5-INGREDIENT
Couscous

Prep Time: 5 mins
Total Time: 17 mins

Servings per Recipe: 4
Calories	239.9
Fat	1.7g
Cholesterol	3.6mg
Sodium	467.6mg
Carbohydrates	46.6g
Protein	9.0g

Ingredients

2 C. chicken stock
1/3 C. currants
1/2 tsp salt
1/8 tsp allspice

1 C. quick-cooking couscous

Directions

1. Place a large saucepan over medium heat. Stir in it the stock, currants, salt and allspice.
2. Cook them until they start boiling.
3. Stir in the couscous and bring them to a rolling boil for 2 to 3 while stirring it them all the time.
4. Turn off the heat and put on the lid. Let the couscous sit for 6 min. Serve it warm or cold with some chopped nuts.
5. Enjoy.

African
Potato Soup

Prep Time: 10 mins
Total Time: 35 mins

Servings per Recipe: 6	
Calories	172.5
Fat	6.3g
Cholesterol	0.0mg
Sodium	812.5mg
Carbohydrates	22.0g
Protein	7.2g

Ingredients

2 tbsp olive oil
1 lb. baby carrots, rinsed
2 medium potatoes, peeled & cut into chunks
1 medium onion, chopped
2 garlic cloves, chopped

6 C. chicken broth
1 tbsp ground cumin
salt and black pepper,

Directions

1. Place a pot over medium heat. Heat in it the oil. Cook in it the garlic, carrots, potatoes, and onion for 6 min.
2. Stir in the broth. Put on the lid and let them cook for 22 min. Allow it to cool down for a while.
3. Get a food processor: Pour in it the soup. Blend it smooth.
4. Pour the soup back into the saucepan. Heat it through for few minutes.
5. Adjust the seasoning of the soup then serve it warm.
6. Enjoy.

TANZANIAN
Banana Curry

Prep Time: 20 mins
Total Time: 1 hr 10 mins

Servings per Recipe: 4
Calories	965.9
Fat	64.9g
Cholesterol	169.6mg
Sodium	845.4mg
Carbohydrates	43.2g
Protein	54.0g

Ingredients

4 tbsp peanut oil
1 (3 lb.) chicken, cut into pieces
1 onion, chopped
2 cloves garlic, chopped
2 tbsp curry powder
1 tbsp dried red chili pepper
2 tsp black pepper

8 C. chicken stock
1 large tomatoes, peeled and chopped
1 C. coconut, grated
2 ripe bananas

Directions

1. Place a large pot over medium heat. Heat in it the oil. Cook in it the chicken pieces for 3 to 5 min on each side.
2. Drain the chicken pieces and place them aside. Stir the onion with garlic into the pot.
3. Cook them for 3 min. Add the powdered chile, the curry, and the black pepper. Cook them for 1 min.
4. Stir in the tomatoes, stock, chicken pieces, and coconut. Cook them until they start boiling.
5. Lower the heat and let them cook for 32 min.
6. Once the time is up, drain the chicken and slice it into strips. Stir it back into the pot and cook it for an extra 12 min.
7. Serve your banana curry warm with some rice.
8. Enjoy.

Nigerian Inspired
Okra

Prep Time: 2 hrs
Total Time: 2 hrs 20 mins

Servings per Recipe: 4
Calories	147.9
Fat	10.3g
Cholesterol	0.0mg
Sodium	11.6mg
Carbohydrates	13.3g
Protein	2.9g

Ingredients

1 lb. young okra pods, trimmed and sliced
2 onions, sliced
3 tbsp olive oil
1/2 tsp dried hot red chili pepper
1/4-1/2 tsp mild curry powder

1/4 tsp ground turmeric
salt and pepper

Directions

1. Get a bowl: Place in it the okra and season it with some salt.
2. Cover it with some cold water. Let it sit for at least 2 h 30 min.
3. Once the time is up, discard the water.
4. Place a pan over medium heat. Heat in it the oil. Cook in it the okra for 11 min.
5. Stir in the onion with chili pepper, curry powder, turmeric, a pinch of salt and pepper
6. Cook them for 4 min. Serve your okra skillet warm with some rice or bread.
7. Enjoy.

CABBAGE
Africano

Prep Time: 5 mins
Total Time: 40 mins

Servings per Recipe: 6
Calories   94.0
Fat   4.9g
Cholesterol   0.0mg
Sodium   104.3mg
Carbohydrates   12.3g
Protein   2.4g

Ingredients

2 - 3 tbsp sunflower oil
1 onion, sliced
1 green bell pepper, seeded and sliced
1 small head white cabbage, sliced
12 ounces canned tomatoes, undrained

1 tbsp mild curry powder
salt
pepper
water

Directions

1. Place a pan over medium heat. Heat in it the oil. Cook in it the onion and pepper for 4 min.
2. Stir in the cabbage, tomatoes, curry powder, tomatoes with juice, salt and pepper. Let them cook for 32 min.
3. Stir in a splash of water. Cook them for 3 to 4 min. Serve your curry warm with some rice.
4. Enjoy.

Brie Stuffed Steak with Rosemary Sauce

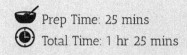 Prep Time: 25 mins
Total Time: 1 hr 25 mins

Servings per Recipe: 4
Calories	1194.3
Fat	87.5g
Cholesterol	329.0mg
Sodium	1478.6mg
Carbohydrates	18.1g
Protein	82.3g

Ingredients

4 thick-cut New York strip steaks
3 heads garlic, halved
1/4 C. olive oil
1 tsp sea salt
3 C. fresh spinach
1/4 C. sun-dried tomato packed in oil, diced
1 lb. fresh brie cheese

1/4 C. fresh rosemary, minced
6 cloves of garlic, chopped
1/4 C. of sour cream
4 tbsp of balsamic vinegar
4 tbsp. of butter

Directions

1. To make the steaks:
2. Coat the steaks with olive oil. Season them with some salt and pepper.
3. Place them in a roasting pan and let them sit in the fridge for an overnight.
4. Before you do anything, preheat the oven to 350 F.
5. Slice the garlic in half and place it in a piece of foil. Drizzle over it some olive oil with a pinch of salt and pepper.
6. Place it in the oven and let it cook for 16 min.
7. Place a pan over medium heat. Heat in it the oil. Cook in it the spinach with chopped tomato and minced rosemary for 3 to 5 min.
8. Turn off the heat and let the mixture cool down.
9. Squeeze the garlic from the peel then add it to the pan with the brie cheese, a pinch of salt and pepper. Mix them well.
10. Use a sharp knife to cut a slit and form a pocket on the side of each steak.
11. Place the filling in each one of them the steak pockets. Use a toothpick to seal them.
12. Before you do anything else, preheat the grill and grease it. Cook on it the stuffed steaks for 4 to 5 min on each side.

13. To make the sauce:

14. Place a small saucepan over medium heat. Heat in it 4 tbsp of butter.

15. Stir in the garlic, 1/4 C. of cream and 4 tbsp of balsamic vinegar. Cook them until the mixture reduces by 1/3.

16. Stir in the rosemary sprigs and cook them for few more minutes.

17. Serve your steaks warm with the rosemary sauce.

18. Enjoy.

Chili Apricots,
Eggplant Curry

🥣 Prep Time: 20 mins

🕐 Total Time: 1 hr 20 mins

Servings per Recipe: 4

Calories	740.4
Fat	35.9g
Cholesterol	127.9mg
Sodium	929.7mg
Carbohydrates	69.6g
Protein	40.5g

Ingredients

3 tbsp cooking oil
2 medium onions, sliced
1 garlic clove, minced
1 small piece fresh gingerroot, peeled and crushed
1 tsp turmeric
1 tsp coriander
1 tsp cumin
1/2 tsp cinnamon
1 1/2 tsp curry powder
1/2 tsp clove
2 lbs. lamb

1/2 lb. eggplant, cubed
1 sweet green pepper, cleaned and chopped
1 - 2 hot green chili pepper
1 C. dried apricot, soaked in warm water and drained
6 ounces tomato paste
1 tsp vinegar
2 C. beef broth
1/2 C. apricot jam
1 C. plain yogurt

Directions

1. Place a pan over medium high heat. Heat in it the oil. Cook in it the garlic with onion and spices for 3 min.
2. Add the spices and cook them for an extra minute. Stir in the lamb and cook them for 8 min over low medium heat.
3. Stir in the rest of ingredients aside from the jam and yogurt.
4. Put on the lid and let them cook for 60 min over low heat. Add the yogurt and jam.
5. Let the stew cook for 3 to 4 min. Serve it warm with some rice.
6. Enjoy.

BASMATI
and Lentils

Prep Time: 10 mins
Total Time: 1 hr

Servings per Recipe: 4	
Calories	562.2
Fat	25.5g
Cholesterol	0.0mg
Sodium	1758.7mg
Carbohydrates	67.6g
Protein	16.4g

Ingredients

1 C. green lentil
1 C. basmati rice
1/2 tsp cinnamon
1/2 tsp allspice
1/4-1/2 tsp black pepper

3 tsp salt
3 3/4 C. water
1 onion, chopped
7 - 8 tbsp olive oil

Directions

1. Place a pan over medium heat. Heat in it 3 tbsp of oil. Cook in it the onion for 4 min.
2. Stir in the spices with lentils and water. Cook them until they start boiling.
3. Lower the heat and put on the lid. Let it cook for 22 min.
4. Stir in the rice with a pinch of salt and pepper. Cook them for an extra 22 min.
5. Once the time is up, serve your lentils stew warm with some ketchup or tomato sauce.
6. Enjoy.

Hummus
Africana

Prep Time: 10 mins
Total Time: 15 mins

Servings per Recipe: 1
Calories	808.5
Fat	51.4g
Cholesterol	0.0mg
Sodium	1112.6mg
Carbohydrates	78.0g
Protein	18.8g

Ingredients

1 (1 1/2 lb.) eggplants, trimmed and cut into pieces
1/3 C. olive oil
1/2 tsp kosher salt
1/4 tsp black pepper, ground
1 (15 ounce) cans chickpeas, drained and rinsed

1/3 C. loosely packed fresh flat-leaf parsley
1 large lemon, juice
2 garlic cloves, minced
1/4 tsp cumin
3 tbsp tahini paste

Directions

1. Before you do anything, preheat the oven to 450 F.
2. Line up a baking tray with parchment paper or foil. lay on it the eggplants.
3. Pour over them some olive oil, a pinch of salt and pepper. Cook them in the oven for 22 to 26 min.
4. Place them aside to cool down completely.
5. Get a food blender: Place in it the eggplant with the remaining ingredients aside from the olive oil.
6. Blend them smooth. Add the olive oil in a steady stream while blending them.
7. Season the hummus with some salt and pepper. Serve your dip with some bread, chips or veggies.
8. Enjoy.

ALEXANDRIA
Rice Casserole

Prep Time: 10 mins
Total Time: 30 mins

Servings per Recipe: 4
Calories   522.0
Fat   19.3g
Cholesterol   31.4mg
Sodium   226.2mg
Carbohydrates   77.2g
Protein   12.0g

Ingredients

1 small onion, sliced
4 garlic cloves, crushed
2 small oranges, grated and juiced
1.5 oz. unsalted butter
1 cinnamon stick
8 oz. long-grain white rice
2 bay leaves
2.6 oz. sultanas

1/2 tsp turmeric
2 1/2 C. chicken stock
1 tsp sunflower oil
1.5 oz. pistachios, shelled
3 sprigs fresh coriander

Directions

1. Place a deep skillet over medium heat. Heat in it the butter. Cook in it the garlic with onion for 3 min.
2. Stir in the rice with cinnamon stick then cook them for 3 min.
3. Stir in the bay leaves with orange zest, orange juice, sultanas, a pinch of salt and pepper.
4. Combine the turmeric with stock. Stir it into the rice pan. Cook them until they start boiling.
5. Lower the heat and put on the lid. Let them cook for 16 min.
6. Stir in the pistachios and cook them for an extra 2 min. Serve your rice casserole warm
7. Enjoy.

Moroccan Lentil
and Za'atar Tagine

🥣 Prep Time: 20 mins
🕐 Total Time: 1 hr 5 mins

Servings per Recipe: 4
Calories   414.9
Fat   8.1g
Cholesterol   15.2mg
Sodium   299.7mg
Carbohydrates   68.9g
Protein   21.2g

Ingredients

2 tbsp butter
2 medium onions, diced
2 small fresh chili peppers, sliced
1 tbsp paprika
1/2 tsp cayenne pepper
1 tsp ground cumin
1 C. dried lentils
4 tomatoes, peeled, seeded and chopped
1/4 C. tomato puree
1 C. chickpeas, cooked

1 C. carrot, diced
1 1/2 C. green beans, cut into pieces
1 zucchini, diced
3/4 C. frozen green pea
1/2 C. flat leaf parsley, chopped
1 tbsp za'atar spice mix, see appendix
salt and pepper

Directions

1. Place a large saucepan over medium heat. Heat in it the oil.
2. Cook in it the onion with chilies for 11 min. Stir in the paprika, cayenne and cumin. Cook them for 1 min.
3. Stir in the lentils with tomatoes, tomato puree and enough water to cover them. Let them cook for 22 min over low heat.
4. Stir in the chickpeas, carrots, green beans, zucchini, and green peas. Cook them for 12 to 16 min.
5. Serve your lentil stew warm with some rice.
6. Enjoy.

SOUTH AFRICAN
White Fish Curry

Prep Time: 5 mins
Total Time: 30 mins

Servings per Recipe: 2
Calories	138.9
Fat	7.3g
Cholesterol	0.0mg
Sodium	1177.3mg
Carbohydrates	17.9g
Protein	2.7g

Ingredients

1 tbsp vegetable oil
2 onions, sliced
3 garlic cloves, crushed
1 tsp curry powder
2 tomatoes, sliced
1 tsp tomato puree
1 tbsp fresh coriander, chopped
1 lb. fish, filleted

1 tbsp lemon juice
1 tsp salt
1/2 C. water

Directions

1. Place a pan over medium heat. Heat in it the oil. Cook in it the onion for 5 min.
2. Stir in the curry powder with garlic. Cook them for 40 sec.
3. Stir in the tomatoes, tomato puree, and fresh coriander. Let them cook for 1 min.
4. Stir in the fish, lemon juice, salt, and water. Put on the lid and cook them for 17 to 21 min over low heat.
5. Serve your fish curry warm with some rice.
6. Enjoy.

Cinnamon
Yam Cookies from Mali

Prep Time: 20 mins
Total Time: 35 mins

Servings per Recipe: 1
Calories	48.7
Fat	1.3g
Cholesterol	7.9mg
Sodium	81.7mg
Carbohydrates	8.5g
Protein	0.7g

Ingredients

1 C. mashed sweet potato
1/4 C. milk
1 egg, slightly beaten
4 tbsp melted butter
1 1/4 C. sifted flour
2 tsp baking powder

1/2 C. sugar
1/2 tsp salt
1 tsp cinnamon
1/2 C. raisins

Directions

1. Before you do anything, preheat the oven to 375 F. Line up a baking sheet with parchment paper.
2. Get a mixing bowl: Beat in it the sweet potatoes, milk, and melted butter with a hand mixer until they become smooth.
3. Add the rest of the ingredients and combine them well.
4. Use a tbsp to drop mounds the batter on baking sheet. Place the sheet in the oven and let them cook for 16 min.
5. Enjoy.

SOUTH AFRICAN
White Fish Curry

🥣 Prep Time: 5 mins
🕐 Total Time: 30 mins

Servings per Recipe: 2
Calories	138.9
Fat	7.3g
Cholesterol	0.0mg
Sodium	1177.3mg
Carbohydrates	17.9g
Protein	2.7g

Ingredients

1 tbsp vegetable oil
2 onions, sliced
3 garlic cloves, crushed
1 tsp curry powder
2 tomatoes, sliced
1 tsp tomato puree
1 tbsp fresh coriander, chopped
1 lb. fish, filleted

1 tbsp lemon juice
1 tsp salt
1/2 C. water

Directions

1. Place a pan over medium heat. Heat in it the oil. Cook in it the onion for 5 min.
2. Stir in the curry powder with garlic. Cook them for 40 sec.
3. Stir in the tomatoes, tomato puree, and fresh coriander. Let them cook for 1 min.
4. Stir in the fish, lemon juice, salt, and water. Put on the lid and cook them for 17 to 21 min over low heat.
5. Serve your fish curry warm with some rice.
6. Enjoy.

Cinnamon Yam Cookies from Mali

🥣 Prep Time: 20 mins
🕐 Total Time: 35 mins

Servings per Recipe: 1
Calories	48.7
Fat	1.3g
Cholesterol	7.9mg
Sodium	81.7mg
Carbohydrates	8.5g
Protein	0.7g

Ingredients

1 C. mashed sweet potato
1/4 C. milk
1 egg, slightly beaten
4 tbsp melted butter
1 1/4 C. sifted flour
2 tsp baking powder

1/2 C. sugar
1/2 tsp salt
1 tsp cinnamon
1/2 C. raisins

Directions

1. Before you do anything, preheat the oven to 375 F. Line up a baking sheet with parchment paper.
2. Get a mixing bowl: Beat in it the sweet potatoes, milk, and melted butter with a hand mixer until they become smooth.
3. Add the rest of the ingredients and combine them well.
4. Use a tbsp to drop mounds the batter on baking sheet. Place the sheet in the oven and let them cook for 16 min.
5. Enjoy.

GARBANZO
Bean Pie

Prep Time: 5 mins
Total Time: 1 hr 5 mins

Servings per Recipe: 10
Calories	174.8
Fat	12.6g
Cholesterol	18.6mg
Sodium	719.3mg
Carbohydrates	10.7g
Protein	4.7g

Ingredients

2 C. chickpea flour
4 C. water
1/2 C. oil
1 tbsp salt
1/4 tsp black pepper

1 egg, beaten
ground cumin
harissa, see appendix

Directions

1. Before you do anything, preheat the oven to 375 F. Grease a baking sheet and place it aside.
2. Get a mixing bowl: Use a hand mixer to blend in it the flour, water, oil, salt and pepper.
3. Pour the mixture into the green pan. Top it with the beaten egg.
4. Place the pan in the oven and let it cook for 65 min.
5. Serve your chickpea tart warm or cold with some ketchup or tomato sauce.
6. Enjoy.

Nkemjika's
Yam Dump Dinner

🍲 Prep Time: 15 mins

🕐 Total Time: 8 hrs 15 mins

Servings per Recipe: 8

Calories	259.4
Fat	8.1g
Cholesterol	0.0mg
Sodium	255.4mg
Carbohydrates	42.6g
Protein	7.1g

Ingredients

1/2 C. small dried red beans
1 large onion, chopped
2 large red bell peppers, chopped
3 garlic cloves, minced
2 tbsp fresh ginger, minced
2 lbs. yams, peeled and cubed
3 C. vegetable stock
2 large tomatoes, diced
1 - 3 jalapeno pepper, minced

1/2 tsp salt
1/2 tsp ground cumin
1/2 tsp ground coriander
1/4 tsp ground cinnamon
1/4 tsp ground black pepper
1/4 C. creamy peanut butter
1/4 C. dry roasted peanuts
1 lime, wedges

Directions

1. Mix all the ingredients in a crock pot except of the peanut butter and roasted peanuts.
2. Put on the lid and let them cook for 9 h on low.
3. Ladle some of the stew stock into a mixing bowl. Add to it the peanut butter and mix them well.
4. Stir it back into the stew pot. Spoon the stew into serving bowl.
5. Garnish it with the roasted peanuts then serve it some lime wedges.
6. Enjoy.

AFRICAN DOLMAS
with Lemon Aioli

Prep Time:1 hr
Total Time: 2 hrs 15 mins

Servings per Recipe: 1
Calories	72.2
Fat	5.4g
Cholesterol	23.4mg
Sodium	377.6mg
Carbohydrates	3.5g
Protein	2.5g

Ingredients

Dolmas:
1/3 C. olive oil
1/2 C. onion, chopped
1/2 C. green onion, chopped
1 lb. lean ground lamb
1/2 C. raw rice
2 tbsp pine nuts
1 tsp dried dill weed
1/2 tsp salt
1/8 tsp pepper
water
1 (16 ounce) jars grape leaves, rinsed
and drained

3 tbsp lemon juice
2 tbsp olive oil
Lemon Aioli
2 tbsp butter
3 tbsp flour
1 1/4 tsp salt
1 (10 3/4 ounce) cans chicken broth
3 tbsp lemon juice
4 egg yolks

Directions

1. Place a large pan over medium heat. Heat in it 1/3 C. of oil. Cook in it the green onion with onion for 6 min.
2. Stir in the lamb and cook them for 11 min. Stir in the rice, nuts, dill salt, pepper and 3/4 C. water.
3. Put on the lid and let them cook for 6 min. Turn off the heat and let it cool down completely.
4. Stir in the rice, nuts, dill salt, pepper and 3/4 C. water. Cook them for an extra 11 min.
5. Turn off the heat and let the filling cool down completely.
6. Lay a grape leaf on a shopping board. Place in it 1 tbsp of the lamb filling. Pull the leaf sides into the middle then roll it over the filling.
7. Repeat the process with the remaining filling and grape leaves. Place them in a deep pan.

8. Pour over them the lemon juice, 2 tbsp olive oil and 1 C. cold water.

9. Cook the grape rolls cook until they start boiling. Place a heavy pan on top of it to cover it.

10. Lower the heat and let them cook for 32 min.

11. Place a small heavy saucepan over medium heat. Heat in it 2 tbsp of butter.

12. Mix in 3 tbsp of flour with 1/2 tsp of salt. Add 1 can of chicken broth with 3 tbsp of lemon juice. Mix them well.

13. Bring them to a boil over low heat while stirring them all the time.

14. Get a small mixing bowl: Whisk in it the 4 egg yolks. Add to them a splash of the hot broth mix. Mix them well.

15. Add the egg yolk mixture to the saucepan. Cook them over low heat until they become thick.

16. Serve your stuffed grape leaves with the egg lemon sauce.

17. Enjoy.

ADAKU'S
Yam Fries

Prep Time: 15 mins
Total Time: 50 mins

Servings per Recipe: 8
Calories	223.8
Fat	9.8g
Cholesterol	7.6mg
Sodium	337.4mg
Carbohydrates	32.6g
Protein	2.0g

Ingredients

2 lbs. sweet potatoes, cut into skinny fries
1 C. good quality mayonnaise, divided

1/4 C. barbecue sauce

Directions

1. Before you do anything, preheat the oven to 425 F. Grease a baking sheet and place it aside.
2. Get a mixing bowl: Combine in it the potatoes with 1/2 C. mayonnaise, a pinch of salt and pepper.
3. Pour the mixture into the baking sheet. Spread it in an even layer. Place them pan in the oven and cook them for 22 min.
4. Stir the potato mix and cook them for an extra 16 min.
5. Get a small mixing bowl: Whisk in it 1/2 C. mayonnaise with 1/4 C. barbeque sauce to make the dip.
6. Serve your sweet potato fries with the BBQ dip.
7. Enjoy.

Coconut
Chickpeas

Prep Time: 5 mins
Total Time: 25 mins

Servings per Recipe: 6
Calories	371.0
Fat	13.3g
Cholesterol	0.0mg
Sodium	464.4mg
Carbohydrates	59.8g
Protein	5.2g

Ingredients

2 C. cooked chickpeas, drained
1 tomatoes, chopped
4 whole cloves
2 - 3 garlic cloves, mined

1 1/2 C. coconut milk
1 1/2 tsp ground turmeric
1/2 tsp salt

Directions

1. Place a large saucepan over medium heat. Stir in it all the ingredients.
2. Cook them until they start boiling. Lower the heat and let them cook for 22 min.
3. Serve your chickpea stew warm with some rice.
4. Enjoy.

LUXOR
Lentils Soup

Prep Time: 10 mins
Total Time: 50 mins

Servings per Recipe: 3
Calories	234.9
Fat	1.5g
Cholesterol	0.0mg
Sodium	781.7mg
Carbohydrates	41.0g
Protein	16.3g

Ingredients

1 small onion, chopped
1 C. red lentil
3 3/4 C. vegetable stock
1 tsp salt
1 dash pepper
3/4 tsp cumin

1/2 tsp turmeric
2 tbsp chopped cilantro
1 dash cayenne
2 tsp lemon juice
olive oil

Directions

1. Place a large saucepan over medium heat. Combine in it the onion, lentils, veggie stock, the salt and pepper.
2. Cook them for 32 min. Add the cumin, turmeric, cilantro, cayenne, and lemon juice.
3. Cook them for 1 to 2 min. Serve your soup warm with a swirl of olive oil and some lime wedges.
4. Enjoy.

Casablanca
Couscous

Prep Time: 25 mins
Total Time: 35 mins

Servings per Recipe: 6
Calories	296.0
Fat	5.1g
Cholesterol	0.0mg
Sodium	205.8mg
Carbohydrates	56.7g
Protein	7.2g

Ingredients

2 C. water
1 1/2 C. uncooked couscous
1/2 C. golden raisin
1/2 C. thawed orange juice concentrate
1/3 C. lemon juice
2 tbsp water
2 tbsp olive oil
2 tsp ground cumin
1/2 tsp salt

1/4 tsp black pepper
3 C. chopped roasted boneless skinless chicken breasts
2 C. chopped peeled cucumbers
1 C. chopped red bell pepper
1/4 C. sliced green onion
1/2 C. chopped fresh cilantro
sliced green onion

Directions

1. Place a large saucepan over medium heat. Heat in it the water until it starts boiling.
2. Add the couscous with raisins. Turn off the heat and put on the lid. Let them sit for 6 min.
3. Get a mixing bowl: Whisk in it the orange juice with lemon juice, water, olive oil, cumin, salt and pepper.
4. Add the couscous and raisins mix with the remaining ingredients. Stir them well.
5. Serve your couscous salad with some green onion on top.
6. Enjoy.

LAGOS
Lamb Kabobs

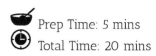

Prep Time: 5 mins
Total Time: 20 mins

Servings per Recipe: 4
Calories   511.7
Fat   36.4g
Cholesterol   120.0mg
Sodium   97.5mg
Carbohydrates   12.5g
Protein   33.6g

Ingredients

Marinade
1 tsp garlic, chopped
2 tsp fresh ginger, chopped
2 tbsp lemon juice
1/4 C. peanut oil
1/2 tsp ground turmeric
1/2 tsp ground coriander
1/2 tsp ground cumin

1/8 tsp cayenne
1 tbsp grated onion
Skewers
2 lbs. lean lamb, diced
2 medium onions, cut into chunks
2 green peppers, cut into chunks
2 tomatoes, cut into chunks

Directions

1. Get a mixing bowl: Combine in it all the marinade ingredients.
2. Stir in the lean lamb dices. Cover the bowl and let them sit for at least 2 h in the fridge.
3. Before you do anything else, preheat the grill and grease it.
4. Drain the lamb dices then thread them into skewers with the onion, pepper and tomato chunks.
5. Place the lamb skewers over the grill. Cook them for 5 to 6 min on each side.
6. Serve your kabobs warm with some bread, your favorite salad and dip.
7. Enjoy.

African Apple
Lamb Meatloaf

🥣 Prep Time: 25 mins
🕐 Total Time: 1 hr 40 mins

Servings per Recipe: 8
Calories   474.5
Fat   33.3g
Cholesterol   135.8mg
Sodium   164.7mg
Carbohydrates   20.0g
Protein   23.3g

Ingredients

3 slices white bread, crusts removed and diced
1 1/2 C. milk
2 tbsp vegetable oil
2 large onions, chopped
1 large carrot, shredded
1 apple, peeled and shredded
1/8 tsp cayenne
1/4 tsp ground coriander
1/3 tsp dry mustard
3/4 tsp turmeric
1/8 tsp ground cloves
1/4 tsp ground cinnamon

1/4 tsp ground cardamom
2 lbs. ground lamb
1/4 C. raisins
1/4 C. mango chutney
1 tbsp apricot jam
1 tbsp white wine vinegar
salt & freshly ground black pepper
2 large eggs

Directions

1. Before you do anything, preheat the oven to 350 F. Grease a loaf pan with a cooking spray. Get a mixing bowl: Stir in it the bread with milk. Let them soak for 16 min. Place a pan over high heat. Heat in it the oil. Cook in it the onion for 3 min. Lower the heat and let it cook for an extra 9 min. Stir in the apple with carrot. Cook them for 4 min. Stir in the spices and cook them for 5 min.

2. Stir in the lamb and cook them for min. Add the raisins, chutney, jam and vinegar. Let them cook for an extra minute.

3. Drain the bread from the milk then add it to the meat mixture. Place the milk aside. Sprinkle some salt and pepper over the lamb mixture. Shape it into a meatloaf and place it in the greased pan.

4. Get a mixing bowl: Beat in it the eggs with milk. Pour the mixture all over the meatloaf.

5. Place the meatloaf in the oven and let it cook in it the oven for 36 min. Enjoy.

BEEF
Liver Skillet (Egyptian)

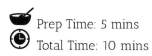 Prep Time: 5 mins
Total Time: 10 mins

Servings per Recipe: 1
Calories   175.5
Fat   12.9g
Cholesterol   137.5mg
Sodium   284.9mg
Carbohydrates   4.0g
Protein   10.5g

Ingredients

17.5 oz. sliced beef liver
1/2 C. cooking oil
1/2 lemon
1 pinch salt
4 garlic cloves
2 chili peppers
1 tsp salt
1 tbsp cumin

1/2 C. vinegar
1 lemon, juice
some cold water

Directions

1. Combine the garlic with chili peppers, salt, cumin, vinegar and lemon juice in a 17 oz. air tight jar.
2. Cover them with cold water. Seal the jar and let them sit in the fridge for several days.
3. Place a pan over medium heat. Heat in it 1/2 C. of oil.
4. Sauté in it the liver with a pinch of salt and pepper for 4 to 6 min or until it is done.
5. Serve your sautéed liver with some bread and pickled chili peppers.
6. Serve it with your favorite toppings.
7. Enjoy.

Coconut
Curried Peas

Prep Time: 5 mins
Total Time: 1 hr 5 mins

Servings per Recipe: 4

Calories	931.3
Fat	25.9g
Cholesterol	0.0mg
Sodium	74.0mg
Carbohydrates	153.0g
Protein	26.7g

Ingredients

1 lb. dried pigeon peas
2 - 3 C. coconut milk
oil
1 - 2 onion, chopped

1 jalapeno, cleaned and chopped
1 tsp curry powder
salt

Directions

1. Place a stew pot over medium heat. Stir in it the peas and enough water to cover.
2. Cook them until they start boiling. Lower the heat and put on the lid. Let them cook until the peas are done.
3. Add 1 1/2 C. of coconut milk. Let them cook over low heat for few minutes.
4. Place a small pan over medium heat. Heat in it a splash of oil. Cook in it the curry for 1 min.
5. Add the chile pepper with onion. Cook them for 3 min. Stir in the peas mixture. Cook them until the veggies are done.
6. Stir in the rest of the coconut milk. Lower the heat and let them let them cook for few more minutes.
7. Serve your peas curry warm with some rice.
8. Enjoy.

SWAHILI
Fried Sweet Bread (Mandazi)

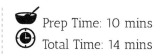

Prep Time: 10 mins
Total Time: 14 mins

Servings per Recipe: 16
Calories   70.2
Fat   0.8g
Cholesterol   12.7mg
Sodium   42.8mg
Carbohydrates   13.3g
Protein   2.1g

Ingredients

2 C. flour
1 1/2 tsp baking powder
1 tsp butter
1 egg, beaten
1/4 C. milk
1/4 C. water

4 tsp sugar
1/4 tsp allspice
vegetable oil

Directions

1. Get a mixing bowl: Combine in it the flour with baking powder, allspice and a pinch of salt.
2. Mix in the sugar with butter until you get a crumbly mixture.
3. Get a mixing bowl: Whisk in it the egg, milk and water. Add it to the flour mix.
4. Combine them well until you get a smooth dough.
5. Place the a large deep skillet over medium heat. Heat in it about 1 to 2 inches of oil.
6. In the meantime, place the dough on a floured board until it become thin.
7. Use a cookie cutter to cut it into your favorite shapes.
8. Place the dough cookie in the hot oil and cook them until they become golden brown.
9. Drain the fried cookies from the hot oil and place them on some paper towels. Dust them with some powdered sugar.
10. Serve your cookies with some chocolate syrup.
11. Enjoy.

Cape Town
Chicken Curry

🥣 Prep Time: 15 mins
🕐 Total Time: 50 mins

Servings per Recipe: 4
Calories	34.7
Fat	0.3g
Cholesterol	0.0mg
Sodium	1169.0mg
Carbohydrates	7.6g
Protein	1.3g

Ingredients

1 medium onion, chopped
2 tsp curry powder
1/2 tsp turmeric
3 ripe tomatoes, chopped
6 pieces chicken
1 1/2 tsp garlic

1/2 tsp ginger
potato, cubed
2 tsp salt

Directions

1. Place a pan over medium heat. Heat in it some oil. Cook in it the onion for 3 min.
2. Stir in the turmeric with curry powder. Cook them for 1 min.
3. Stir in the tomato and cook them for 3 min. Stir in the remaining ingredients.
4. Put on the lid and lower the heat. Let the stew cook for 20 to 30 min until the chicken is done.
5. Enjoy.

2-INGREDIENT
Plantains

Prep Time: 2 mins
Total Time: 27 mins

Servings per Recipe: 4

Calories	218.3
Fat	0.6g
Cholesterol	0.0mg
Sodium	7.1mg
Carbohydrates	57.0g
Protein	2.3g

Ingredients

4 plantains, in their skins
cooking spray

Directions

1. Before you do anything, preheat the oven to 400 F. Line up a baking tray with parchment paper.
2. Lay in it the plantains. Cook them in the oven for 22 to 26 min until they become soft.
3. Remove the plantains from the oven. Serve them right away with some ice cream.
4. Enjoy.

Moroccan Honey
Pomegranate Salad

Prep Time: 15 mins
Total Time: 15 mins

Servings per Recipe: 4
Calories	274.8
Fat	12.8g
Cholesterol	0.0mg
Sodium	59.9mg
Carbohydrates	38.5g
Protein	6.8g

Ingredients

4 oranges, peeled, deseeded, cut into pieces
1/2 C. pomegranate seeds
1 tbsp orange zest
1/2 C. almonds, chopped
1/4 C. pistachios, chopped

3 tbsp honey
1 tbsp water
cinnamon

Directions

1. Get a mixing bowl: Toss in it the oranges, pomegranate seeds, almonds and pistachios.
2. Get a microwave safe bowl. Place it in the microwave and cook it for 35 sec.
3. Drizzle the honey dressing over the salad. Stir it to coat.
4. Garnish the salad with some orange zest and cinnamon then serve it.
5. Enjoy.

HOT ZUCCHINI
Tunisian

🍲 Prep Time: 15 mins
🕐 Total Time: 25 mins

Servings per Recipe: 3
Calories   111.8
Fat   9.4g
Cholesterol   0.0mg
Sodium   34.8mg
Carbohydrates   6.7g
Protein   1.4g

Ingredients

1/2 lb. zucchini, slice
2 - 3 carrots, sliced
Dressing
2 tbsp olive oil
1 garlic clove
1/2 tbsp harissa, see appendix
1/4 tsp ground cumin
1/4 tsp caraway seed

juice of half lemon
Topping
plain yogurt
fresh cilantro
salt,
cracked black pepper

Directions

1. Get a mixing bowl: Mix in it the all the marinade ingredients. Toss in it the veggies.
2. Cover the bowl with a plastic wrap. Place it in the fridge for 65 min.
3. Before you do anything, preheat the grill and grease it. Lay the veggies slices on the grill.
4. Cook them for 2 to 4 min on each side until they are done.
5. Serve them with your favorite dip.
6. Enjoy.

Madagascar
Coconut Stew

🥣 Prep Time: 10 mins
🕐 Total Time: 50 mins

Servings per Recipe: 4
Calories	260.6
Fat	10.3g
Cholesterol	65.8mg
Sodium	101.9mg
Carbohydrates	14.0g
Protein	28.6g

Ingredients

2 (1/2 lb.) boneless skinless chicken breast halves, cut into pieces
2/3 C. coconut milk
1 1/2 C. yellow onions, chopped
1 bell pepper, chopped
3 garlic cloves, minced

2 tsp ground ginger
1 lemon, juice and zest
1/3 tsp cayenne, adjust
salt and pepper

Directions

1. Get a mixing bowl: Toss in it the chicken with lemon juice. Let them sit for 35 min.
2. Drain the chicken pieces. Toss them with some salt and pepper.
3. Place a pan over medium heat. Heat in it the oil. Cook in it the chicken pieces for 8 min.
4. Drain the chicken pieces and place them aside. Stir the onion into the pan and cook it for 3 min.
5. Stir in the garlic with bell pepper. Cook them for 4 min.
6. Lower the heat then stir in the coconut milk, ginger, cayenne powder, cooked chicken and grated lemon zest.
7. Put on the lid and let them cook for 32 min. Serve your chicken stew with some rice.
8. Enjoy.

SOMALI
Flatbread

Prep Time: 10 mins
Total Time: 13 mins

Servings per Recipe: 8
Calories	200.6
Fat	3.8g
Cholesterol	0.0mg
Sodium	147.1mg
Carbohydrates	35.7g
Protein	4.8g

Ingredients

3 C. flour
1 -1 1/2 C. water
1/2 tsp salt,

2 tbsp oil

Directions

1. Get a mixing bowl: Mix in it the oil with flour and salt. Mix in the water until you get a smooth dough.
2. Place the dough ball in a greased bowl. Brush it with some oil and cover it. Let it rise for 30 min.
3. Shape the dough into 8 balls. Lay each dough ball on a floured surface. Flatten it into an 8 inches circle and coat it with some oil.
4. Pull the edges of the dough circle into the middle pinching them in the center in the shape of square.
5. Repeat the process with the remaining dough.
6. Place a griddle over medium heat. Brush the dough squares with some extra oil.
7. Cook them in the hot pan for few more minutes on each side until they become golden brown.
8. Serve your golden bread warm or cold.
9. Enjoy.

African
Caprese Appetizer

Prep Time: 8 mins
Total Time: 28 mins

Servings per Recipe: 3

Calories	431.3
Fat	29.9g
Cholesterol	37.8mg
Sodium	602.9mg
Carbohydrates	31.0g
Protein	12.7g

Ingredients

4 - 6 large tomatoes, sliced
1 tsp dried basil
1/2 tsp flaked sea salt
4 - 6 tbsp tomato ketchup
4 ounces brie cheese, sliced
1/2 tsp black pepper

1 red onion, sliced
4 - 6 tbsp virgin olive oil
3 - 4 slices bread, crusts cut off

Directions

1. Before you do anything, preheat the oven to 350 F. Grease a baking dish with some oil.
2. Lay in it half of the tomato slices. Top it with the basil, 3 tbsp of ketchup, salt and pepper.
3. Top it with half of the cheese slices. Repeat the process to make another two layers.
4. Pour over them some olive oil. Lay the onion slices on top followed by the bread slices
5. Drizzle over them some extra olive oil. Place the pan in the oven and let them cook for 22 to 26 min.
6. Serve your Caprese tart warm.
7. Enjoy.

YAM
Breakfast Pancakes

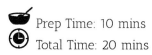

Prep Time: 10 mins
Total Time: 20 mins

Servings per Recipe: 4
Calories	372.0
Fat	11.9g
Cholesterol	143.7mg
Sodium	118.4mg
Carbohydrates	54.1g
Protein	11.7g

Ingredients

3 eggs, lightly beaten
1/2 C. milk
2 tbsp olive oil
1 1/4 C. flour
12 ounces sweet potatoes, peeled and grated

2 onions, sliced
2 tsp dried thyme
sunflower oil
salt
pepper

Directions

1. Get a mixing bowl: Whisk in it the eggs, milk and olive oil. Add the flour and mix them well until no lumps are found.
2. Mix in the sweet potatoes, onions, thyme, a pinch of salt and pepper.
3. Place a large pan over medium heat. Heat in it splash of oil.
4. Use a ladle to pour some of the mixture into separate circles. Cook them for 2 to 3 min on each side.
5. Repeat the process with the remaining mixture until all the cakes are done.
6. Serve your yummy cakes with your favorite dip.
7. Enjoy.

Stuffed Peppers
North African

Prep Time: 25 mins
Total Time: 1 hr 15 mins

Servings per Recipe: 8
Calories	394.7
Fat	21.7g
Cholesterol	115.1mg
Sodium	676.6mg
Carbohydrates	32.2g
Protein	18.6g

Ingredients

8 medium bell peppers
1 1/2 lbs. lean ground lamb
1 large onion, chopped
2 C. cooked rice
1/2 C. ketchup
1/2 C. raisins
1 tsp ground allspice
1/2 tsp ground cumin

1/2 tsp ground cinnamon
1/2 tsp black pepper
2 eggs, lightly beaten
1 1/2 tsp salt
1/4 tsp cayenne pepper

Directions

1. Before you do anything, preheat the oven to 375 F.
2. Cut off the bell peppers tops and reserve them. Discard the seeds and membrane of the peppers.
3. Place a pan over medium heat. Cook in it the lamb for 6 to 8 min. Discard the fat.
4. Stir in the onion with chopped pepper. Cook them for 6 min. Turn off the heat.
5. Mix in the rice, ketchup, raisins, allspice, cumin, cinnamon, black pepper and eggs to make the filling.
6. Adjust the seasoning of the filling then spoon it into the bell peppers.
7. Place the stuffed peppers in a greased casserole pan. Cover them with their cut up tops.
8. Lay a loose piece of foil over the stuffed peppers. Cook them in the oven for 42 to 52 min. Serve them warm.
9. Enjoy.

DICED POTATOES
and Spinach Congolese

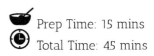
Prep Time: 15 mins
Total Time: 45 mins

Servings per Recipe: 4

Calories	822.8
Fat	56.3g
Cholesterol	0.0mg
Sodium	386.3mg
Carbohydrates	72.1g
Protein	11.7g

Ingredients

4 potatoes, diced
2 C. spinach, washed, chopped
1 C. oil
4 garlic cloves
2 C. garbanzo beans
1 red pepper, seeded, diced
1 green pepper, seeded, diced

1 medium onion, peeled and chopped
1 tsp oregano
2 tsp dried basil
Topping
ground cayenne pepper

Directions

1. Place a large saucepan of water over medium heat. Bring it to a boil.
2. Cook in it the potato dices for 9 min. Stir in the spinach and cook them until they are done.
3. Pour the potato and spinach in a colander. Let them dry for few minutes.
4. Place a large pan over medium heat. Heat in it the oil. Cook in it the spinach and potato for 5 to 7 min.
5. Stir in the reaming ingredients, with a pinch of salt and pepper. Cook them for 4 min.
6. Serve your potato stir fry warm with some rice.
7. Enjoy.

Homemade
Harissa

Prep Time: 20 mins
Total Time: 20 mins

Servings per Recipe: 40
Calories   28 kcal
Fat   2.8
Carbohydrates   0.9g
Protein   0.2 g
Cholesterol   0 m
Sodium   176 mg

Ingredients

6 oz. bird's eye chilies, seeded and stems removed
12 cloves garlic, peeled
1 tbsp coriander, ground
1 tbsp ground cumin
1 tbsp salt
1 tbsp dried mint
1/2 C. chopped fresh cilantro

1/2 C. olive oil

Directions

1. Add the following to the bowl a food processor: chilies, cilantro, garlic, salt mint, coriander, and cumin.
2. Pulse the mix until it is smooth then add in some olive oil and pulse the mix a few more times.
3. Place the mix in jar and top everything with the rest of the oil.
4. Enjoy.

HOMEMADE
Harissa
(Tunisian Style)

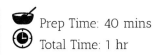

Prep Time: 40 mins
Total Time: 1 hr

Servings per Recipe: 192
Calories   10 kcal
Fat   0.3 g
Carbohydrates   1.9g
Protein   0.4 g
Cholesterol   0 m
Sodium   26 mg

Ingredients

11 oz. dried red chile peppers, stems removed, seeds, removed
3/4 C. chopped garlic
2 C. caraway seed

1/2 tsp ground coriander seed
2 tsps salt

Directions

1. Let your chilies sit submerged in water for 30 mins then remove the liquids.
2. Now add the following to the bowl of a food processor: salt, pepper, coriander, garlic, and caraway.
3. Puree the mix then place everything into a Mason jar and top the mix with a bit of oil.
4. Place the lid on the jar tightly and put everything in the fridge.
5. Enjoy.

Za'atar
Spice Mix

🥣 Prep Time: 5 mins
🕐 Total Time: 5 mins

Servings per Recipe: 1
Calories	367.8
Fat	28.3g
Cholesterol	0.0mg
Sodium	18621.4mg
Carbohydrates	25.4g
Protein	11.7g

Ingredients

4 tbsps ground sumac
2 tbsps whole thyme
3 tbsps toasted sesame seeds
2 tbsps oregano
2 tbsps ground marjoram

1 tsp savory
1 tsp basil
2 tbsps kosher salt

Directions

1. Get a food processor or blender and add the following to it: sumac, thyme, sesame seeds, oregano, marjoram, savory, basil, and salt.
2. Pulse the mix for a few mins until everything is smooth.
3. Add the mix to a storage container.
4. Enjoy.

ALTERNATIVE
Za'atar
(No Sumac)

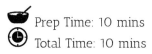 Prep Time: 10 mins

Total Time: 10 mins

Servings per Recipe: 1
Calories   746.0
Fat   61.7g
Cholesterol   0.0mg
Sodium   5251.4mg
Carbohydrates   39.1g
Protein   22.8g

Ingredients

3 tbsps toasted sesame seeds
2 tbsps thyme
1 tbsp marjoram
1/2-1 tbsp finely grated lemon zest

1 tsp kosher salt

Directions

1. Place your toasted sesame seeds into a blender. Work the mix into a smooth powder.
2. Get a bowl, and add in your: powdered sesame seeds, thyme, marjoram, lemon zest, and salt.
3. Stir the mix completely, then pour everything into storage containers.
4. Enjoy.

Mango
& Raisin Chutney

Prep Time: 20 mins
Total Time: 1 hr 5 mins

Servings per Recipe: 1
Calories   627.2
Fat   2.1g
Cholesterol   0.0mg
Sodium   3748.7mg
Carbohydrates   153.4g
Protein   4.2g

Ingredients

1 kg very firm mango
2 C. sugar
625 ml vinegar
1 (5 cm) pieces ginger, peeled
4 cloves garlic, peeled

2 - 4 tsps chili powder
4 tsps mustard seeds
8 tsps salt
1 C. raisins or 1 C. sultana

Directions

1. Peel the mango and then remove the pit and chop it.
2. In a pan, add sugar and vinegar, leaving about 20ml and simmer, stirring occasionally for about 10 minutes.
3. Meanwhile in a food processor, add remaining vinegar, garlic and ginger and pulse till a paste forms.
4. Transfer the paste into a pan and simmer, stirring continuously for about 10 minutes.
5. Stir in the mango and remaining ingredients and simmer, stirring occasionally for about 25 minutes or till desired thickness of chutney.
6. Transfer the chutney into hot sterilized jars and seal tightly and keep aside to cool.
7. This chutney can be stored in dark place for about 1 year but remember to refrigerate after opening.

TANGY
Fruit Chutney

Prep Time: 25 mins
Total Time: 40 mins

Servings per Recipe: 1
Calories	456.6
Fat	5.7g
Cholesterol	0.0mg
Sodium	171.9mg
Carbohydrates	105.8g
Protein	2.5g

Ingredients

1 lb fresh cranberries
2 1/2 C. sugar
1 C. water
1/2 tsp salt
1/2 tsp ground cinnamon
1/2 tsp ground cloves
1 medium onion, chopped

1 medium tart apple, peeled and cubed
1 medium pear, peeled and cubed
1 C. raisins
1/4 C. lemon juice
1/2 C. chopped walnuts

Directions

1. In a large pan, add cranberries, water, sugar, spices and salt on medium-high heat and bring to a boil.
2. Reduce the heat to low and cook, stirring occasionally for about 10 minutes.
3. Stir in pear, apple and onion and cook for about 5 minutes.
4. Remove from heat and immediately, stir in lemon juice and raisins.
5. Transfer the chutney into a bowl and refrigerate for at least 8 hours.
6. While serving, fold in walnuts.
7. Enjoy with a dressing or meat of your choice.

Plum-Ginger
Chutney

Prep Time: 20 mins
Total Time: 1 hr 10 mins

Servings per Recipe: 1
Calories   567.7
Fat   1.0g
Cholesterol   0.0mg
Sodium   1190.1mg
Carbohydrates   142.6g
Protein   2.4

Ingredients

3 1/2 C. purple plums, seeds removed
1 C. brown sugar
1 C. sugar
3/4 C. cider vinegar
1 C. golden seedless raisins
2 tsps salt
1/3 C. chopped onion

1 clove garlic, minced
2 tsps mustard seeds
3 tbsps chopped crystallized ginger
3/4 tsp cayenne

Directions

1. In a large nonreactive pan, mix together vinegar and sugar and bring to a boil.
2. Cook, stirring continuously till sugar is dissolved completely.
3. Stir in the remaining ingredients and bring to a boil.
4. Reduce the heat to low and cook, stirring occasionally for about 40-50 minutes or till desired thickness of chutney.
5. Transfer the chutney into hot sterilized jars and seal tightly and keep aside to cool.
6. For better taste use after about 1 month.

ENJOY THE RECIPES?

KEEP ON COOKING
WITH 6 MORE FREE COOKBOOKS!

Visit our website and simply enter your email address to join the club and receive your 6 cookbooks.

http://booksumo.com/magnet

https://www.instagram.com/booksumopress/

https://www.facebook.com/booksumo/

Printed in Great Britain
by Amazon